D1645560

HOUSE OF PLANTS

HOUSE OF PLANTS

Living with succulents, air plants and cacti

Caro Langton & Rose Ray

CONTENTS

THE
HOUSE

Every plant has a story.

House of Plants began with an empty home full of memories – a miracle of a space that had belonged to my grandmother, on the edge of Hampstead Heath in north London.

When Rose and I unexpectedly found ourselves the guardians of this house, we discovered we had also inherited a collection of ancient cacti, succulents and tropical plants, all comfortably settled in their found positions as if their roots were bound to the surfaces they sat upon. Occupying unused places, from brightly lit windowsills to the darkest forgotten corner of a bedroom, the plants seemed to inhabit each space as if they were always meant to be there. By noting their conditions, we began to identify why each one was surviving seemingly so effortlessly.

Although we had both grown up with naturally green-fingered parents, neither Rose nor I had qualifications in gardening or botany. But tucked away in the study (lined with tropical William Morris wallpaper) we found a library of gardening books, and we eagerly began reading about our new green friends. The key for us was observation and coming to understand the signs that meant it was time to attend to each one. As our confidence grew, we sought new species to add to the family, from air-cleansing tropical palms to gravity-defying air plants. Some thrived and others didn't. We soon learned which were the most suitable for different indoor conditions.

As the house began to breathe with a weird and wonderful selection of flourishing plants, we started to experiment with new and unexpected ways to house each one. Rose, a creative through and through, began casting concrete pots, cutting glass and designing terrariums to hold little pockets of tropical greenery. Hidden away inside a cocoon of English ivy, our conservatory began to transform into a mosaic of foraged objects, a glimmering sea of antique glass vessels and battered trays filled with crystals. Surrounded by a tangle of soldering guns and teacups, Rose would emerge each day with something new for me to quickly steal to photograph and share online. Together we experimented with metals and cut copper tubes, forming geometric shapes to suspend our favourite air plants.

Eventually we took an assortment of curious objects and plants to sell at Broadway Market in east London hoping that other people would share our enthusiasm. From that first sunny Saturday, there was an immediate sense of kinship with the people met from all walks of life. The plants we had nurtured were connecting us to strangers in ways we could never have imagined, and we felt suddenly bound to these botanicals. With encouragement from our customers we started running workshops, styling shop interiors and weddings, and creating products to help people to make their own indoor gardens. This was the beginning of our company, which we called Ro Co.

THE
STORY

Growing up, I was enchanted by tales of faraway lands. I spent much of my time outdoors imagining the characters from the books I loved living happily among my mum's plants. Our garden was a stretch of overgrown wilderness, intensely green and untamed, and the plants indoors were equally wild and carefree: dotted around rooms, between stacks of books, they were an extension of the verdant landscape I was lucky enough to be surrounded by.

My parents had an elderly gardener who I rarely saw, but who attempted to control the space as best he could: new passageways would appear through the waist-high grass after school for me and my sister to explore. I remember the first time we saw the Chilean giant rhubarb which sprung from a damp patch at the very bottom of the garden and running our hands over its leathery leaves, each the size of an umbrella. After being cut back and covered in a blanket in the autumn, it would revive itself as if by magic each spring and we would crouch underneath it, hidden and slipping deep into the world of childhood imagination.

Cut flowers can be beautiful, of course, but to me they have always felt unnatural indoors, suspended for a moment in a forced composition before being quietly disposed of, their drooping heads shedding petals all the way to the dustbin. For me, greenery in a home should be in motion, breathing, changing, promising life and growth. I feel genuinely connected to indoor plants in a way I never could to a bouquet of flowers.

My first real experience of tropical plants was at school, which was next door to a small botanical garden. Once we were old enough, we were allowed to escape for an hour each day into the refuge of the tropical glasshouses. The chatter of birdsong was enchanting, while the clinging humidity would make us sweat in our polyester school uniforms amid the towering bird of paradise plants.

Much later, while living with my grandmother in her house in north London, I fell in love with her collection of cacti and succulents, each one so distinctly settled in its spot. She had a wonderfully wicked sense of humour. I have particularly fond memories of her fluffy old man cactus, subtly named Hairy Dick, which we would rotate monthly to ensure he grew upright. I remember the year he proudly flowered in pink, which caused something of a celebration. She was also someone who saw the beauty in every chipped ornament and battered kitchen utensil and her approach to indoor gardening was similarly relaxed: hastily arranged tangles of wild flowers from her garden mingled with potted tropical plants and succulents. From the ethereal dracaena corn plant that tickled the ceiling of one hallway to an ancient spider plant, confidently flinging out new shoots in the corridor outside my bedroom, her plants were a reflection of her calm and resourceful nature.

From her I learned to appreciate the beauty of improvisation.

In another part of rural England, Rose was experiencing a similarly green youth, one interwoven with family adventures outdoors. Having trained as a garden designer, Rose's mum encouraged her to spend as much time outside as possible, be it the rich expanse of woodland which framed the small farm they lived on, or the fascinatingly diverse gardens of Tresco in the Isles of Scilly where they went on holiday.

At home, she would forage and save little pieces of the landscape while out on her childhood adventures, returning with pockets full of acorn kernels, lichen, skeleton leaves and cracked pieces of flint to arrange in the garden under an elderly laurel tree. One day, while exploring the nearby Haleacre Wood, she discovered an old diary concealed under the fallen leaves – amid the private pages, elaborate stories were conjured of its owner who had found solace among the same trees many years before her. The distinct smells of each season were memorable too: lingering scents of pine sap, decaying leaves, hay, buttercups and freshly cut nettles, which remained with her long after she left home.

It was the concept of rehoming something in an unlikely way that first captivated Rose's imagination. Coming across an antique cine camera lens at a flea market, she was drawn to its shape, but more importantly the way the curved glass created an otherworldly feel. She took it apart and arranged within it a collection of sea-worn flint, pyrite, quartz and dried lichen, attempting to capture the essence of the landscape inside the previously abandoned object. Rose soon began working as a set designer, finding new opportunities to silently convey a unique story with the help of many combined elements. Every detail was significant, and she gradually learned how to transform an interior space. Hoping to turn this passion into a way of life, she sought ways to create objects for other people to enjoy in their homes. The answer came with a visit to San Francisco's Mission District, where she immediately connected with the area's alliance between nature and urban life.

The variety of unusual flora was overwhelming: collections of sun-soaked succulents lining shop windows, and doorways framed in shaded jungle greenery. From giant potted plants to repurposed, ancient-looking terrariums tucked away in protected spaces, the city's love for plants (and the sense of well-being they helped foster) seemed to radiate from the candy-coloured streets of each neighbourhood.

Returning with a fresh sense of purpose, Rose began sourcing exotic plant life that, with a little encouragement, could thrive within the landscape of any loving home. With our shared mantra of 'more green', I quickly joined her, and we set out on our goal to fill as many spaces as we could with unusual, beautiful plant life.

THE
PHILOSOPHY

'There is something so basic, so natural in the hand that the urge to utilise its power will always make itself felt.' – **YANAGI SOETSU**

Both of us have backgrounds in design, so an important part of our journey has been making or sourcing objects that aim to support and nurture our plants. To feel the weight of a hand-thrown ceramic pot, noticing with each turn the marks of its maker traced on its textured surface, is to feel a personal connection to the joy of a thoughtful process. Buying a plastic flowerpot from a garden centre inspires little less than indifference. The beauty of a handmade possession is not just in its unique quality or considered nature, but in knowing that there is a personal story behind its creation. For us, this is the magic element which gives authenticity to any product.

More and more we see people finding fulfilment and pride in living with objects and belongings that have been made and chosen with consideration. And as a society, we seem to be actively searching for chances to learn and appreciate practical skills that reflect a more thoughtful mindset and help reduce the effects of excessive consumerism. Perhaps the joy of being resourceful, and the sense of achievement that brings is helping to slowly close the void between manufacturer and consumer.

There is a strange belief that when designing you should keep the process a secret for fear of others copying. We have found the opposite to be true and are happy to admit that we have been inspired every day by our customers, friends and other designers. In fact, some of the best ideas we have developed grew from conversations and suggestions from those we have met since we began our business, simply by asking for advice or sharing thoughts with strangers.

Throughout this book, you will find **YOU | CREATE** guides, where we have shared projects we love such as a simple macramé hanging planter (p135), tropical terrarium (p67) and our lightweight concrete pot recipe (p79). The projects are simple, inexpensive and teach practical skills that will help you make the most of your living space and create unusual ways to display your favourite plants. Feel free to change or add to the basics we run through in this book, and try experimenting with your own unique designs.

We hope that you can take your time transforming your home into a house of plants and find pleasure in all the little details. We hope, too, that you experience the same satisfaction in sustainable design that has so encouraged us on our journey.

LIVING WITH
PLANTS

A home is a sanctuary: a familiar landscape, a sheltered meeting place with both light and dark, a unique expression of ourselves.

Rose and I met during our final year at university. Life was hectic and spontaneous, and to be truthful we had little time or money for indoor plants. 'Green' was limited to half-empty Fairy liquid bottles and the mould-patterned bathroom ceilings of decaying rented houses. There was a disconnect between 'home' and where we were living, but that was part of what made the experience of university so liberating. It was only after settling in London and finding ourselves once again with limited living space, but this time with stability and a little money to furnish our house, that we began to create a real home that meant something to us. For us both, this meant more green.

However, life in the city doesn't always allow for straightforward indoor gardening. Moving between rented properties (which often don't have a kitchen table, let alone room for repotting), many of our customers tell us that they would love to fill their homes with greenery, but simply don't have the space. We believe part of the satisfaction of living with indoor plants is in their modest requirements, and just as much pleasure can be found in a humble potted cactus as in a conservatory full of demanding tropical plants. With this in mind, we have covered all types of species that will thrive in very different conditions, from a brightly lit windowsill to a shady bookshelf.

For many of our friends, regular travelling means that they are wary of adopting plants when they cannot guarantee they can give them the attention they deserve. Included in this book are specifically low-maintenance species that we have discovered on our journey.

From the forest-dwelling tillandsia, which we used for our first commissioned window display, to the air-purifying tropical plants which nurture us as we nurture them, we have selected only plants which are easy to find and difficult to kill.

No matter where you find yourself calling home, we believe creating your own pocket of green doesn't have to be complicated. Once you identify the basic needs of each plant you choose to live with, we hope you find the same sense of achievement that we did in creating an environment of growth in your home that is as hassle-free as possible.

KNOWING YOUR PLANTS

cacti, succulents, air plants,
tropical plants & their needs

Just as we found ourselves the unexpected guardians of a house full of plants, it's likely your indoor greenery will find you when you are least prepared: given as gifts, or perhaps stealing your attention while strolling through a local market. These surprise acquisitions are the plants we fall instantly in love with, chosen solely for their irresistible charm or given to us out of love. It will only be after you get them home that you start to think about the prime spot to display them and the conditions they might need to thrive.

Luckily, most indoor plants are surprisingly adaptable, and unless they are subjected suddenly to extreme abuse they will give you clear warning signs that they are unhappy. Often we care for our plants a little too enthusiastically, and the most common cause of death is, tragically, overwatering.

This chapter aims to help you familiarise yourself with the different families of plants suitable for indoor living and the signs that tell you when each one is blooming or suffering. We have included most of the questions our customers frequently ask us, such as how much light each requires, when to water, and how best to deal with a plant that becomes unwell. Once you have learned about the origin, characteristics and growth cycles of each family, as well as choosing the right living conditions for the plants you decide to bring home, caring for each one will become second nature.

PLANTS YOU'LL MEET

USEFUL TERMS

ACTIVATED CHARCOAL

A form of crushed charcoal which can filter toxins from water. Often used to prevent bacteria growing inside a terrarium

ACTIVE GROWTH PERIOD

The period when a plant grows new leaves and flowers, typically between early spring and late summer

AREOLE

The unique organ of the cactus family, producing spines, flowers and offsets

COIR

A fibrous, absorptive material produced from the husk of coconut shells. Can be mixed with compost to help preserve moisture

EPIPHYTE

A plant that takes root on the body of another plant or tree

FAMILY

A group of plants which contains one or more genera, e.g. Crassulaceae

GENUS

A classification of plants within a family, each containing one or more different species, e.g. Echeveria

OFFSET

A new plant produced organically by a parent plant, often at its base, which can be removed for propagation

PERLITE

Lightweight expanded volcanic glass used to assist drainage in compost

PINCHING

A method of pruning a plant's stem with the finger and thumb in order to encourage new growth lower down

REST PERIOD

The period between the end of summer and the start of spring when a plant is inactive, producing little new growth

ROCK DUST

Finely crushed volcanic rock containing a high level of essential minerals and elements. Often added to compost to aid plant health

SPECIES

A set of plants within a single genus, with similar characteristics and the ability to interbreed, e.g. *Echeveria elegans*

TERRARIUM

A fully or partially sealed transparent container in which plants are grown

TOPDRESS

To apply a top layer of fresh compost to a potted plant as an alternative to repotting the entire plant

VARIEGATED

Flowers or leaves showing an unusual pattern of different colours or marks

VERMICULITE

A mineral used to assist drainage and retain nutrients and moisture in compost

WORM CASTINGS

An enriching form of organic fertiliser made from (highly nutritious) worm poo

MAKING PLANTS FEEL AT HOME

You want to make your plants feel at home, placed in conditions that are at least partly similar to their native environments. Species of tropical plants are so readily available that it is easy to forget their needs and instead feel overcome with the beauty of delicate stems and multicoloured leaves. Plants inspire emotion, and although the idea of rehoming an exotically foliaged friend is hard to resist, there is something crushing about having to dispose of it a few weeks later when it suddenly keels over and starts to rot.

Take a moment to stand in any room of your home: observe the way the light falls, notice the sources of warmth, look for the shady spots, or perhaps identify a draught from a window or doorway. Consider appliances like radiators and ovens – these are likely to suddenly alter the temperature and humidity of the environment. Stand and take note again later in the day, when the conditions will have changed, sometimes quite significantly.

When it is in its ideal position, a plant will be at its attention-grabbing, animated best and it will thrive when it is getting just the right amount of love from you that it needs. Therefore when you first pick up a plant, it is worth thinking realistically about whether it can happily survive in your home and around your schedule.

With the majority of the plants featured in this book, the most important factors to consider are light and watering requirements. For example, succulents rely on lots of direct sunlight to stay healthy, so if your home has little natural light it is perhaps better to avoid collecting these. Tropical plants typically need to be watered once a week, sometimes more in warmer months, so may not be suitable for those who travel a lot (this includes the rubber plant *Ficus elastica* pictured on the right and p143). You can find advice on keeping tropical plants alive while you are on holiday on p62.

Although our customers range from first-time plant owners to experienced indoor gardeners, most tend to be looking for 'low-maintenance' plants to decorate their homes and suit their busy lives. With this in mind, we have made sure to include a selection of species to suit different kinds of domestic conditions and lifestyles. By recognising the places in your home that could be suitable to introduce greenery, you can then explore the various plants that will flourish there.

More specific information on the most appropriate plants to choose can be found in the House of Plants chapter on p123, which also offers inspiration on how to style and display many of our favourite species.

BRINGING PLANTS HOME

Sourcing and selecting unique plants is part of the fun of filling your home with greenery. From specialised nurseries and indoor flower markets to our green-fingered friends' homes, there are so many places we look out for unusual species to adopt.

Although many succulents are happy to live outdoors in warmer climates, we generally avoid buying tropical plants or air plants that have been displayed outdoors. This is especially the case in winter months, when they are likely to have been damaged by the cold.

It sounds obvious, but when you spy a plant you like, the first thing to do is to have a quick look at its tag, which will give some idea of its lighting and watering requirements. This is your first opportunity to decide whether it's right for you. If you are taking a cutting from a friend (see p99) consider whether the plant is thriving where it is currently placed and whether you have similar light and temperature conditions at home.

With all plants, look out for brown, patchy, drooping or dropping stems and leaves, which can be signs of disease. If it's potted, check that the soil looks fresh and fills the pot, with no signs of mould or limescale. If there are roots escaping from the bottom of the pot, the plant is probably due to be repotted, so consider whether you are willing to tend to it immediately or if you would rather choose one with more space to grow in its current pot.

Before leaving a shop or nursery, make sure your plants are properly packed up to protect them from being knocked and damaged. Wrapping them in a protective layer of paper or tissue will also prevent them from sudden cold draughts, which can cause them to become unwell before you have even got them through your front door. This is specifically important for delicate tropical plants that are prone to reacting badly to extreme changes in temperature.

We have suffered many a pricked body part in our time, so if you know you are going out to buy cacti, take a little cardboard box to bring them home in. Taller cacti can often be top-heavy and are much more delicate than they look. If you buy a larger cactus, make sure it is packaged in a thick-walled box and cushioned with scrunched-up newspaper to avoid any snapped spines.

Finally, bear in mind that tropical plants often need a period of time to acclimatise to new living conditions. For the first week or so after placing your new plant in a suitable space, it may show worrying signs such as wilting a little or dropping some of its leaves. As long as it is protected from direct light or heat, it is better to leave it alone and keep its soil moist, giving it the chance to settle rather than rushing to find a better spot.

CACTI & OTHER SUCCULENTS

Native to far-flung regions including the arid grasslands of South Africa, the rainforests of Madagascar and the deserts of Patagonia and Mexico, the variety of these water-storing plants seems almost endless. From the stout and prickly to the trailing and elegant, the diversity of the succulent family makes them irresistible to collectors.

Having adapted to areas prone to drought, a succulent is the name given to any plant that stores reserves of water in its leaves or stems. Therefore, all cacti are succulents. Some species of succulents masquerade as cacti, though, and the two can sometimes be confused.

The easiest way to tell if a succulent is a cactus is by looking for what botanists call 'areoles' – little round bumps on the surface of the plant where a cactus produces its spines and flowers.

There are two different kinds of cacti – desert and forest – and they must all have areoles to be classified as one. You can tell whether your cactus is native to arid (desert) or tropical (forest) regions by looking at its stem shape. Because they need to store more water to survive, desert cacti are often bulbous, columnar, or flat and cylindrical, and have interesting spines. Forest cacti, which mainly grow as epiphytes, often trail or branch out in spineless stem formations and are used to dappled rather than direct light. Forest cacti such as the fishbone cactus (p184) can have less obvious areoles, often positioned along the edges of its stems. Rather than having leaves, desert cacti have spines that protect the plants from predators and help to reduce loss of water.

Other popular succulent plants include agaves, sedums, lithops and crassulas, and all of these genera are native to semi-desert regions. They often have juicy leaves and distinct flowers and are ideal for children since they are so easy to care for. Like desert cacti, they require as much direct sunlight as possible to thrive, so are suited to the brightest locations in your home. But despite their distant origins, succulents show an incredible willingness to adapt to urban living, happily surviving after being left home alone for a month or two without being watered, even accepting an occasional run-in with a window blind or inquisitive cat with casual dignity.

If you are just setting out on your plant journey, succulents are a great place to start. They are resilient and require similar living conditions to each other, making it easier to choose plants you are drawn to solely for their beauty or colour. Be warned, though; their variety makes them addictive. We often have serious conversations with our customers about an obsessive urge to gather more and more – confessions of skin dotted with spines, houses taken over by aloes and echeverias, and their growth documented and discussed as if they were pets from outer space.

LIGHT

With the exception of forest cacti (see p29 for the difference between forest cacti, desert cacti and other succulents), succulents require direct light, so should be placed on the brightest surfaces of your home. This is doubly important in the winter, when natural light may be limited. In the summer, you can pop all your succulents outside to get fresh air and as much light as possible. Bear in mind that forest cacti should never be placed in strong direct sunlight, as they will quickly overheat and die. If your home has little natural light, look for species from the rhipsalis, hatiora and epiphyllum genera, which all like indirect light.

Indoors, it is normal for natural light to fall on one side of a plant, leaving the other side in shade. So to prevent distorted growth, remember to rotate succulents regularly.

Keep in mind that once a plant has acclimatised to a spot, it might change if suddenly moved to a much brighter position, so look out for signs of yellowing or withering, which could indicate sun damage.

TEMPERATURE

During their active growth period (in spring and summer), succulents require warm indoor temperatures during the day (about 18–30°C/65–85°F). However, their native conditions (very hot days and cold nights) mean they can cope with cooler night temperatures as long as they have received adequate sunlight during the day. This makes them suitable for most people's homes.

During their rest period (from autumn until the start of spring), you can keep succulents in cooler living conditions (about 10–13°C/50–55°F) as long as they continue to receive direct light. Make sure to protect them from frosts and draughty windows. They must be kept dry in order to survive the colder months. But be aware of very dry conditions caused by heaters (or air conditioning during the summer), which may affect how often you need to water your plants.

HUMIDITY

Since they are native to typically arid environments, most succulents thrive in warm, dry conditions with little humidity. All plants benefit from fresh air and succulents are no exception. On hot summer days, give your succulents lots of ventilation by opening windows and doors. Forest cacti also like good ventilation and should be put outside periodically in warmer months, as long as they are protected from direct light.

FLOWERING

Many cacti and succulents flower indoors during their active growth period, even from a young age. Certain cacti bloom at night and their flowers can be any hue except for blue. Although the flowers of many cacti are often spectacularly colourful, don't be fooled by the rainbow coloured blooms miraculously adorning trays of miniature cacti at flower markets – they are likely to be attached with a sneaky dab of glue. Commonly found forest cacti such as species of rhipsalis, which are used to shady conditions, will also gladly flower indoors without direct light.

Since there are so many plants classified as 'succulent', do a little research on a specific species to find out more about its flowering characteristics as well as the best ways to encourage each one to bloom in your home. Also see the House of Plants chapter on p123 for more on individual plants.

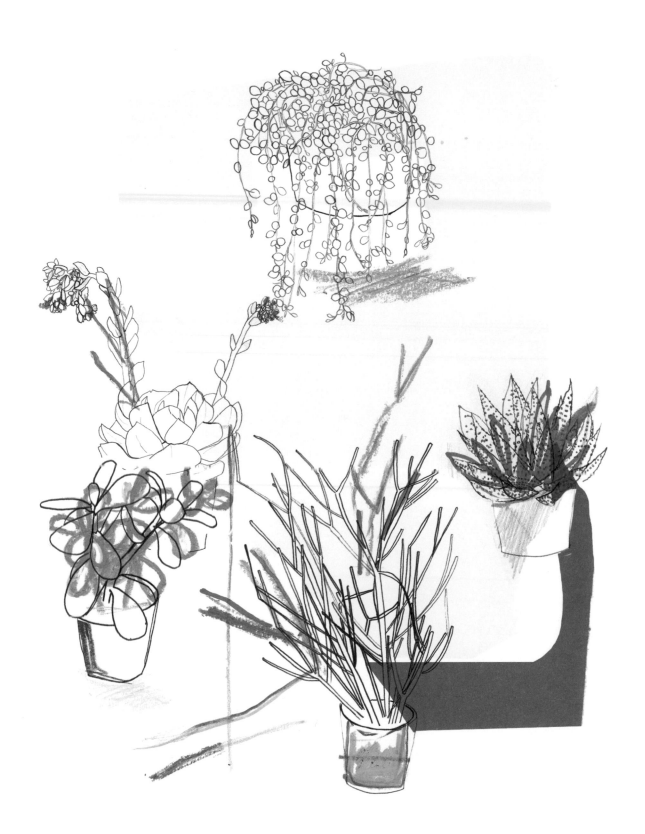

ASTROPHYTUM
myriostigma

ASTROPHYTUM
ornatum

ASTROPHYTUM
...atum x

WATERING

{ cacti & other succulents }

It is easy to assume that cacti and other succulents require very little water since they are so well adapted to store moisture. But just like any other plant they need regular access to water in order to survive, especially during their active growth period. For succulents, this is from early spring until the end of the summer, when they can be watered as often as a couple of times a week, provided they have adequate drainage and light.

In spring and summer, you can tell when to water a succulent by testing the moisture level of its soil with your finger. When the top 3cm/1½in of the plant's soil feel completely dry, it is time to water. Since the majority of these plants are native to sandy desert regions with very good drainage, it is important that the soil is allowed to dry out before you water it again. And make sure to water in the morning to ensure excess moisture has time to drain before night-time.

During winter months, when succulents enter a period of rest, you can reduce watering as they require significantly less moisture to survive. Succulents kept in a greenhouse won't need watering at all during their rest period, but in heated (and therefore very dry) rooms of your home they should be watered only when their soil dries out completely. When watering, do so in the mornings so excess moisture has time to drain before nightfall. Giving them too much water when they are inactive can cause bacteria to form in their roots as the water will sit and stagnate rather than absorb.

The exception to this rule is forest cacti, which require watering throughout the year. You can test the soil as normal with your finger, watering only when the top 3cm/1½in are completely dry. After a forest cacti flowers, give it a few weeks' rest before watering it again.

The ideal watering technique is to stand the plant pot in a tray, then add water to the tray. Allow the plant to absorb water through the pot's drainage holes until the surface of its soil becomes damp to the touch. At this point, remove the pot from the tray so that the plant's roots never sit in water for a prolonged period of time. Too much water can damage the fine hairs on the roots, eventually restricting its ability to absorb moisture. If you have lots of succulents, you can use a long watering tray to make this routine less time-consuming. If you find water isn't being absorbed, you can also water your succulents from above with a spouted watering can. Succulents are used to sudden bursts of water after severe drought in their natural habitat, so this won't harm them.

A couple of last things to note: plants in plastic pots retain more moisture than those in clay pots, so less frequent watering might be required. And if you live in a hard-water area, use filtered water or rainwater at room temperature to ensure optimum plant health.

FOR THE FORGETFUL | *If you neglect a succulent for a long time, its soil becomes brittle and withdrawn from the edge of its pot. Before watering, loosen the soil with your fingers to make sure the water doesn't run straight out of the bottom.*

PRUNING
& CARE

{ cacti & other succulents }

It's always wise to handle a cactus or succulent with care, no matter how harmless or hardy they look. You may do damage to them, and equally the most innocent-looking species can cause skin irritation and pricks. Waxy-leaved succulents, including certain species of echeveria, can be bruised if their leaves are handled. Cacti with very fine bristles such as the opuntia or prickly pear easily shed their spines and penetrate skin. When removing a spiky cactus from its pot, you may need a pair of thick gloves to protect your hands. Alternatively, scrunch up a few sheets of newspaper until thick enough to wrap around the spines without piercing your skin. More help with repotting can be found on p84–91.

PRUNING

Cacti generally need little in the way of pruning, except after they have finished blooming. At this time, the dried flowers can be gently removed. Leafy succulents shed their leaves quite regularly and any older, withered leaves or flowers can simply be plucked off to improve the look of the plant. When pruning a leafy succulent, remember that any healthy stems or leaf cuttings removed to improve its shape (or by accident) can be easily propagated rather than thrown away. See the Sharing Your Plants chapter on p99.

CLEANING

Inevitably, your indoor plants will gradually pick up dust on their surface, which can inhibit their growth. In the case of a prickly cactus, you may see little bits of loose soil caught up in its spines, especially if it has just travelled home with you. For prickly desert cacti, use a soft, dry paintbrush to stroke away any dirt or dust. For forest cacti or other spineless succulents, you can gently clean them with a damp cloth or sponge, taking extra care with more delicate leaves and stems.

FEEDING

When grown indoors, succulents are likely to mature slowly and therefore require little fertiliser to survive. However, if you would like to encourage a succulent to flourish and flower, use a diluted houseplant fertiliser regularly from early spring to late summer (but never during winter months when the plant is in its rest period). Try making your own nettle fertiliser using our recipe on p95. Specific instructions for how often to feed different species can be found on each plant focus page in the House of Plants chapter on p123.

COMMON
AILMENTS

{ cacti & other succulents }

WILTING

It's a common misconception (especially if you are a new succulent owner) that the wilting of stems or leaves is due to a lack of water. In fact, it is more likely to be a symptom of over-zealous watering. Roots will become damaged, preventing the succulent from absorbing the moisture it needs to survive and causing it to wilt. Another common symptom of overwatering is a gradual yellowing of its leaves, so if they are wilting and yellow, you can be pretty sure of the problem.

If your succulent starts to look wilted, take it out of its pot and check how wet its soil is. If the soil is very dry, give it a gentle watering so as not to shock it, then see if its appearance improves after a day or so. If the soil is damp, leave the plant for a few weeks and only give it more water once the soil is completely dry. For more advice on watering, see p35.

SHEDDING LEAVES

The loss of leaves can be caused by a few different issues, from unusually high temperatures to damage from harsh pesticides. The most common cause, though, is underwatering, which causes succulents to self-prune their leaves to conserve energy. If it slips your mind sometimes, set yourself a reminder and adjust your watering routine.

Just bear in mind that dry, crispy leaves at the bottom of a plant are normal in a healthy, growing succulent, and these can be pruned to encourage new growth. Also, most healthy sedums will naturally shed their fleshy leaves to self-propagate, so do not worry too much if you notice healthy-looking leaves dropping from lower down the stem of this genus.

TREATING UNWELCOME PESTS | *Pests indoors are relatively rare (compared to myriad outdoor pests), but occasionally a succulent may encounter a family of marauding bugs. Most likely it will be the mealy bug, which resembles a small, white woodlouse. Mealy bugs set up home in tiny nests between the plant's leaves and roots, and these look like little pieces of cotton wool. Individual bugs can be removed with a fine paintbrush. Then roots should be checked for signs of further infestation. If you identify an infestation, you can make your own, non-toxic insecticide by mixing 1 litre of water with 1tsp organic neem oil and ¼tsp mild liquid soap, and gently spraying affected areas of the plant. Make sure to do a small spot test on the plant first to check it won't react badly to the solution.*

SUDDEN WITHERING AND YELLOWING OF LEAVES

Although succulents are not prone to attacks by pests, beware of mealy bugs and slugs, especially if you place your succulents outdoors in warmer months. If you suspect your plant may be under attack, check its soil for signs of the mealy bug (see note on p39). You can treat any infestation by cutting away affected parts of the roots and repotting the plant in fresh potting mixture, then keeping a close eye on it.

PALE LEAVES AND SPINDLY STEMS

Succulents with insufficient light will grow long and pale, often with yellow, stunted leaves. Notably, succulents such as echeverias may grow long, spindly stems to search for a better source of sunlight (see p102 for ways to propagate an unsightly succulent). Cacti will elongate and become soft. Moving your plant to a spot where it receives more light will usually restore it to health.

SOFT, BROWN AREAS

Soft, brown areas are normally due to rot from severe overwatering, which damages roots. Succulents are especially vulnerable to bacteria, so will begin to rot if too much moisture builds up around their roots or leaves. If you notice rotten areas on your plant, cut the damaged flesh away to prevent bacteria spreading, and then reduce frequency of watering (for more advice on watering, see p35). If the rot is very severe, you may need to cut off any healthy green tissue that remains and propagate these sections in fresh soil, most likely with either leaf or stem cuttings. See the Sharing Your Plants chapter on p99 for help.

DARK, DRY PATCHES

These can be caused by over-handling, particularly if apparent in more delicate cacti and succulents. But dark patches can also be the result of scorching if the plant is put outside or in front of a window in very intense sunlight. If your succulent is very mature, dark patches around the base of the plant may simply be an indication of its age. Although unsightly to some, dry patches will not spread and should be treated as marks of your plant's long and eventful life.

NO GROWTH

This is likely to be due to underwatering in warmer months or overwatering in winter. It could also be due to stunted growth if you have not repotted your plant for a very long time, or are keeping it in a very small pot. For help with how and when to repot, see the Nurturing Your Plants chapter on p73.

A NOTE ON REPOTTING | *To avoid a build-up of moisture in your pot and therefore root rot, always repot succulents in the spring or summer when necessary. At this active stage in their growth cycle, repotting is a good way to remove old, nutrient-lacking soil and replenish your plant with fresh nutrients to promote growth. When repotting a succulent, a layer of small stones at the bottom of the pot is essential for good drainage and maintaining healthy roots. See the Nurturing Your Plants chapter on p73 for a guide on how, when and why to repot.*

AIR
PLANTS

Imagine a room where the plants are suspended, defying gravity, thriving on every and any surface. Unrooted and independent, they hang from the ceiling, freely live along bookshelves and float in front of every wall. This is how our studio has come to be and it is possible to achieve this in your home too, with a little bit of imagination.

When we first became familiar with air plants, we had never seen them displayed indoors. We had seen them in the public conservatories we had visited, where we were transfixed by swathes of trailing Spanish moss, and intrigued by the occasional, unexpected rosette of leaves attached curiously to the branches of larger tropical trees. We thought them unusual, but hadn't realised their potential as houseplants. Then Rose visited San Francisco: here, she discovered a selection of air plants in an indoor gardening shop, perched casually between books and antique ornaments. She was instantly captivated, and began to source them for us to experiment with. Since then, they have become our favourite family of plants to display, somehow balancing beautifully between delicacy and resilience.

Air plants, or tillandsia, are a genus of over 500 species of evergreen plants from the bromeliad family. In the wild, they generally grow as epiphytes, anchoring themselves with roots to other plants and trees for support. Their diversity is an indication of their widespread origins, from the forests of Florida, through Mexico and Guatemala, and all the way down to the mountainous and desert regions of Argentina and Chile in South America.

Amazingly, despite their diverse natural habitats, air plants as a whole require little care. This is partly because they are such slow growers: their sculptural leaves appear almost in a state of paralysis. However, it is a common mistake to think that air plants need only air to live. In fact, they survive in the wild by absorbing moisture and nutrients through their leaves, which are hugely varied in shape, size and colour. Because of this, they do not require roots or soil, and only need minimal watering or pruning to live indoors.

When displaying them, remember they require a good flow of air between their leaves, so enclosed containers or surfaces that absorb or contain water should be avoided. Certain metals can be toxic to them, so choose clear fishing wire or threads to suspend them instead.

Air plants are also fantastic houseplants for children, since they are so low maintenance and are unbothered by being handled. Though they are not toxic to pets, be aware of cats, who love to steal them for their own pleasure.

LIGHT

A few species of air plants, such as the xerographica (p202), require direct light, but almost all other species are suited to bright, indirect light. This is because they have adapted to the strong but dappled light they received in their native habitats where they would seek support from other plants and trees that partially blocked the sun. This makes them great for displaying in most rooms of the home – just avoid putting them on brightly lit windowsills in summer months, where they may scorch, shrivel and become dehydrated.

TEMPERATURE

Any warm room temperature is suitable in the day, in the range of 10–30°C / 50–85°F, and cooler night-time temperatures are fine for most species. If you choose to display an air plant in a warm room, you may need to increase the frequency of watering to ensure it stays hydrated. Although they are generally very hardy, make sure to protect them from frosts in colder months, which can shock them and cause them to die suddenly. Never expose your air plants to draughty conditions or very low temperatures, particularly if they are damp (from watering, for example), as this can cause them irreversible damage.

HUMIDITY

Depending on their natural habitat, certain species of air plants prefer different levels of humidity. See p51 for more on where your air plants might originally be from, or go to the House of Plants chapter on p123 to identify which rooms may be best for them.

FLOWERING

During spring and summer months, many mature air plants begin to flower, sending out a long stalk called an 'inflorescence' between the middle of their leaves. The flowers are often vibrant shades of pink, violet and yellow. With the right lighting conditions, certain species such as the ionantha will 'blush', its leaf tips (or even the whole plant) turning red before flowering.

The species we have found most likely to bloom include the ionantha, butzii and xerographica (p202). The ionantha can flower every 9 months, but the flowers are short-lived. The xerographica flowers less regularly, but each psychedelic bloom can last up to a year.

After flowering, air plants typically produce offsets, or 'pups', and then gradually begin to fade, but this can take many months. The offsets can be left attached to form a cluster of new plants, or removed to live independently as new plants. See p114 for more on this.

FAILURE TO FLOWER | *All species of air plants flower, but many take years before they are mature enough to do so. You can encourage your plants to bloom by supplementing their water with a liquid seaweed fertiliser high in nitrogen, and by providing them with their optimum light and temperature needs.*

Knowing Your Plants

WATERING

{ *air plants* }

We genuinely enjoy watering our air plants. Our customers admit the same: watching a collection of these alien-like plants bob around in a tub, their colour immediately deepening as the filaments on the surface of their leaves become saturated, is a strangely enchanting experience. Although the watering requirements of different species of this genus are quite similar, it is interesting to identify where each of your air plants come from before deciding on a watering routine.

Thinner, greener-leaved species are often native to wetter habitats such as rainforests, where they don't need to store as much water to survive. This type of air plant dries out quickly indoors, so soak at least once every week. They also enjoy a regular misting and are happily displayed in more humid rooms such as kitchens and bathrooms. Species included in this group are the butzii, caput-medusae (pictured top right and p171), bulbosa (pictured bottom left and p173) and Spanish moss (p207).

Air plants with thicker, often silvery leaves are likely to be native to arid regions, where their leaves adapted to act as a reserve when rainfall is limited. Their silver colour is due to tiny hairs (trichomes) which reflect light and absorb extra moisture. These species are the hardiest and prefer to be kept in rooms with low humidity and a good air flow to avoid a build-up of moisture between leaves. They are happiest when soaked roughly once a week, with an occasional misting in warmer weather. The xerographica (p202), ionantha and oaxacana (pictured top left and p205) are some of the most commonly found species in this category.

Having said this, one of the wonderful things about air plants is that it is very unlikely you will kill them by overwatering alone. Whether you choose to spray or soak them, they will draw up only as much moisture as they need, so in general you can water liberally without any worry of harming them. In warmer months, or if your home is particularly dry, we suggest watering all air plants at least once a week, and more if they look dehydrated. See p54 for common signs of dehydration.

There are two golden rules when watering air plants – ignore either and you might be causing irreversible damage. The first is to gently shake off any excess moisture after watering. This is to prevent rot forming between the leaves, which can happen quite quickly with the limited air flow in most people's homes. Alternatively, leave your air plants to dry on a surface upside down, so that any excess water can easily drain away. Air plants should be watered before midday, encouraging them to dry off as quickly as possible before night-time, otherwise a chill could lead to long-term damage.

The second rule is to use the right water to keep them healthy. Try to use water at room temperature to mimic these plants' natural conditions. If you live in a hard-water area, the levels of calcium in tap water can eventually cause the air plant's trichomes to become damaged. Rainwater is excellent and you can collect it outside in a bucket to be transferred to a spray bottle for misting or a small bowl for soaking. If you are unable to collect rainwater, use bottled or filtered water. In soft-water areas, you can simply run air plants under tepid tap water.

PRUNING
& CARE

{ *air plants* }

PRUNING ROOTS

Air plants may produce fine, wiry roots as they seek to anchor themselves for support. These can be trimmed away without causing the plant any harm.

SHEDDING LEAVES

Air plants produce new leaves from their centre, so it is normal for the older, outer leaves to gradually dry out and drop off. You can remove any dry leaves by gently pulling them downwards, but stop if you feel any kind of resistance, as this means the leaf is still healthy. If your air plant is shedding lots of leaves, it is likely due to unsuitable light, temperature or humidity. See p46, then perhaps find a new place to display your plant.

CURLING LEAVES

This is typically a sign of dehydration and indicates that you need to water your plant more frequently. See p51 for more on how and when to water your air plants.

DRY, BROWN AND SHRIVELLED

If your plant shrivels and dries up, it is probably receiving too much direct light, leading to scorched, damaged leaves. As long as you notice this quickly, you can give it a good watering and move it to a more suitable place. Another cause could be dehydration, in which case you should soak the plant overnight to rehydrate it and begin more frequent watering to restore it to health. Brown leaf tips are often down to underwatering – if the plant seems otherwise healthy, the tips can be trimmed at an angle with scissors to improve its overall look.

SOFT BROWN AREAS AND ROTTING

If you find your air plant suddenly turns brown at the base of its leaves and falls apart, it could be that a build-up of water has led to rot. Sadly, there is nothing you can do to save it at this stage. For future plants, remember to make sure that you allow excess water to drain from the plant after watering. See p51 for more on how and when to water your air plants.

FEEDING

For optimum health, supplement your air plant's water with an organic liquid seaweed fertiliser (which is high in nitrogen) once a month. This will encourage plants to bloom, and improve their growth in general. Bear in mind that too much fertiliser can burn air plants, so dilute it to a quarter of its recommended dosage.

Knowing Your Plants

TROPICAL PLANTS

With their diverse leaf shapes, exotic patterns and depth of colour, indoor tropical plants make a room feel instantly alive. Despite taking up more space than many succulents, their intensity somehow lends a space a sense of openness, almost as if the walls behind them have disappeared. With limited free surfaces in smaller city apartments, they are also a pleasing choice when it comes to filling a vacant corner of a bedroom or living room floor.

Tropical plants grow faster than succulents and air plants, and therefore react to changing conditions quickly too, naturally shifting towards sources of light and warmth, their leaves uncurling and fanning out after each watering. This makes them particularly rewarding to live with, and observing the way they adapt and settle into a room is a satisfying way to feel the benefits of nurturing each one. And they have even more to give: because their leaves have adapted to photosynthesise with reduced sunlight, they purify the air we breathe indoors more efficiently than other indoor plants. In certain cities like Delhi, where air pollution is a major problem, tropical plants such as the areca palm, peace lily and money plant are being grown indoors as they significantly reduce a range of toxins found in the air. In our homes, they remove chemicals such as benzene, formaldehyde and carbon dioxide, giving a generous amount of oxygen in return.

We have focused on species of foliage plants rather than those that are flowering, since they typically need less light to flourish, and have more interesting leaf shapes and patterns. Variegated (coloured) versions of many commonly known tropical plants can be found quite easily – look out for particularly striking hybrids of ficus, philodendrons and aspidistra – but they are typically a little less hardy. Since all of the foliage plants featured in this book are native to subtropic and tropic regions (where they have adapted to dappled light), they are suited to homes with indirect bright light, or even low light conditions.

Bear in mind that tropical plants require more frequent watering than succulents and air plants, although we have featured only the most resilient species. And although they require more maintenance, they are also suitable for rooms which tend to become humid, such as bathrooms and kitchens.

EASY CARE | *For those who find caring for indoor plants a little difficult, we suggest beginning with the forgiving cast iron plant (p130), snake plant (p183) or spider plant.*

LIGHT

The intensity and consistency of light required by tropical plants varies hugely from plant to plant, even within one genus. For example, within the ficus genus, the familiar rubber plant loves to be in indirect light, whereas the creeping fig will only survive in a shady location. As a general rule, most species prefer to be away from direct light, enjoying bright, filtered light.

Since natural light from a window is likely to fall on one side of a plant, leaving the other side in shade, plants should be rotated occasionally to help them grow evenly.

Observe their leaves for clues to whether they are receiving the right amount of light. See p64 for more on the common symptoms of too little or too much light.

TEMPERATURE

The majority of indoor plants will thrive if you provide them with an indoor temperature range of 10-30°C / 50-85°F in the day and cooler temperatures at night. The worst temperature conditions are those that fluctuate. In colder months, protect plants by moving them away from draughty windows and doors, and be aware of radiators and other heating appliances that may alter the temperature of a room dramatically. In summer months, be careful not to shock plants with sudden blasts of cold air from air conditioning systems.

HUMIDITY

Plants in general benefit from having fresh air to breathe, so give tropical plants gentle ventilation through a window every now and again, especially in warmer months when rooms can become stuffy. Certain tropical plants, such as ferns, love high levels of humidity and feel at home in bathrooms. For most tropical plants kept indoors, misting isn't vital, and watering their soil is the best way to keep them healthy.

REST PERIOD | *Although many indoor plants native to temperate climates enjoy a period of rest during winter months, tropical plants are used to less distinguished seasons. Instead they respond to the amount of rainfall they receive, so it is best to reduce the frequency of watering and stop feeding altogether in the winter to encourage a period of rest.*

Just keep an eye out for wilting, which may indicate a gentle watering is needed. You can increase your watering frequency again once you notice signs of growth. This will often kick in as natural light increases at the start of spring, and indicates that your plant is entering its active growth period.

See p61 for more advice on watering your tropical plants.

Knowing Your Plants

WATERING

{ tropical plants }

Tropical foliage plants require quite a bit more attention and hydration than succulents and air plants. But like anything you care for, it can be very satisfying to work their needs into a busy schedule while getting to know each one individually.

The majority of indoor foliage plants need frequent watering between early spring and the end of summer when they are in their active growth period, and they will need significantly less in their resting period during autumn and winter. To judge when it is time to water, check each plant's moisture level by inserting your fingertip into the top of its soil. If the top 3cm/1½in are dry, the plant needs watering.

There are a couple of simple methods of watering which have their own benefits and it is really a matter of finding the one that suits your lifestyle. The fastest method is to use a spouted watering can, taking care not to splash the leaves and stems of the plant. Another method is to water plants from below, which requires a little more patience but tends to be better for the plants. To do this, immerse each pot in a bowl of water so that it can absorb as much moisture as it needs through its drainage hole. Leave it in the bowl until the top of the plant's soil feels damp. Then remove and allow to drain on a saucer or tray. The plant's roots should never sit in water for a prolonged period of time as this can damage them and cause rot. It is best to water them in the morning, allowing the plant to drain excess moisture before night.

While it is important to water only when necessary (rather than as a matter of routine), we find that keeping a topped-up watering can and mister near the pots acts as a visual nudge to water the plants (or at least check if they need watering), and it takes much of the hassle out of the process.

If you live in a hard-water area, use room temperature filtered water or rainwater to prevent long-term limescale or calcium damage. If you live in a soft-water area, you can use tap water, but let it reach room temperature in your watering can first.

For indoor plants that love high levels of humidity, you can also mist their leaves every few days. Use tepid water and mist plants in the morning so that their leaves can dry before nightfall. Misting can also benefit tropical plants by cooling them down on hot summer days, but remember never to mist a plant that is receiving direct light as this can lead to scorched leaves.

Since tropical plants have adapted to thrive in high humidity, during warmer months you can prevent their compost drying out too quickly by sitting each pot on a tray lined with small drainage stones. After watering, excess water will collect in the tray and as it evaporates it will help the compost remain moist without causing a build-up of stagnant water. The level of water should never be higher than the stones, though, as this could be counter-productive and lead to root rot.

PRUNING
& CARE

{ *tropical plants* }

PRUNING

Most indoor foliage plants require little pruning to stay healthy, but an occasional trim can help to promote new growth and encourage fullness, especially in trailing or climbing plants. Look to prune your plants only during their active growth period. When pruning, make a clean cut above a node on the stem, which is the spot where a branch or leaf is attached.

It is perfectly normal for more mature plants to naturally shed their oldest leaves. If you notice dry, brown leaves, you can simply pluck them off to improve the plant's appearance and stimulate new shoot growth. See p64 if you are worried about brown leaves.

CLEANING

As well as dulling the appearance of leaves, dust can reduce the level of light your plant receives and block leaf pores, causing them to stop breathing efficiently. If you notice a build-up of dust on the leaves of your plant, use a clean, damp sponge or cloth to gently wipe them, supporting each leaf with your hand as you go.

FEEDING

Tropical plants delight in being given extra nutrients to encourage their growth and vitality. See p95 for our homemade nettle fertiliser recipe.

HOLIDAY CARE

As long as you can maintain a suitable temperature in your home while you are away, and you remember to give them a generous watering before you go, leaving tropical plants for a week or two during their rest period should cause little harm. In warmer months, leave them well-watered and away from any sources of direct light or heat.

To help reduce water loss, you can line each plant's watering tray with a layer of small stones, which will increase the humidity below the pot. For tropical plants that respond to high humidity, you can encase the entire plant in a spacious plastic bag to prevent dehydration, but this can lead to rot if left for longer than a week or so.

If going away for longer than a week in the spring or summer, line a bucket, sink or bath with very damp newspaper, sitting your well-watered plants on top. Ensure they are protected from direct light and are not in a place where the temperature will fluctuate too drastically. Otherwise, it's far safer to find a plant-loving friend to pay your plants the odd visit while you are away, perhaps tempting them with some stem cuttings in return.

COMMON
AILMENTS

{ tropical plants }

Since there are often multiple reasons for the following symptoms, try not to make any rash responses until you are sure of the most likely cause. Indoor plants can take longer than expected to react to poor living conditions, so when you see a sign that your plant is suffering, think back to the care you have given it in the last couple of weeks before making any diagnosis or treating it.

BROWN, DROPPING LEAVES

Some less resilient tropical plants are more vulnerable to sudden temperature changes caused by draughty windows, air conditioning or fluctuating central heating.

Other culprits behind brown, shedding leaves are underwatering and conditions which are too dry. Make sure you are providing your plant with enough moisture and check whether it might be better suited to another, more humid room. If your home is very dry in general, consider misting the plant daily.

In species that like shady conditions, brown leaves on the top of the plant could suggest too much direct light. In this case, move the plant to a shadier place and prune any dead leaves, giving it a good watering afterwards.

YELLOWING LEAVES

It is normal for a leaf to occasionally turn yellow, but if you notice more yellowing than usual, there are a few causes. Too much calcium in hard tap water, as well as cold draughts damaging leaves are both possible factors. But the most likely cause is an unhealthy watering routine. Since too much and too little water can cause yellowing, check the moisture level of your plant and adjust your routine accordingly. See p61 for more advice on watering.

ROTTING

Rotting is caused by overwatering, or too much humidity in a room. It is hard to treat a plant once rot damages its roots, so prevent the problem by making sure your plant has good drainage, and only water it when the soil feels dry. See p61 for more advice on watering.

LIFELESS, WILTING LEAVES

This is most likely the fault of too much direct light, especially if you notice the leaves wilting during the middle of the day. Another cause is too little water, which you can determine by inserting a finger into the soil to check whether it is dry. The best way to treat this problem is to give your plant a healthy watering and if necessary use a piece of bamboo and some string to gently support the wilted stems. After a week or so, you should notice the plant revive itself and you can return to a normal watering routine.

TROPICAL GLASSHOUSE TERRARIUM

Inspired by the variety of plants we saw at the tropical greenhouses around England, we starting sourcing glass vessels at flea markets and antique fairs, and planting them up in order to decorate the shady spaces around the house where other plants had struggled to survive. Since tropical plants do not like direct light, especially when they are enclosed in glass (which causes condensation to build up), a tropical terrarium is best suited to a shady bookshelf or bedside table. However, they do need some natural light so try not to plunge them into the darkest corner of your home.

Containing plants inside and underneath glass is curiously satisfying – for us it's like creating a miniature other world and a sort of visual storytelling, which takes us back to the innocent enchantment of childhood fairytales. This sense of magic is heightened even more if you decorate your terrarium with crystals (choose chemically inactive forms such as quartz and pyrite) or other found objects.

When it comes to choosing a vessel, you can use anything you find attractive from an apothecary jar or a glass cloche to a small or large aquarium. The sealed or semi-sealed nature of these containers increases the humidity within the glass, creating a contained biosphere that makes it easier to keep more delicate tropical plants alive indoors. We do not recommend enclosing cacti or other succulents in glass, since the levels of moisture will eventually cause them to rot.

Clean your vessel thoroughly before you begin to remove any bacteria that may lead to the growth of mould. If disinfecting, rinse it well and air it outside for a couple of days to avoid harming the plants with chemicals.

With narrow-necked vessels, you can use modified kitchen utensils such as a cork- or tissue-topped chopstick or skewer to help secure and clean each plant once it is in the right position. You can use a spoon as a makeshift spade and a fork as a rake for topdressing. We have found that a long wooden spoon is the most useful tool, since you can use the rounded end to direct soil and stones into hard-to-reach areas, and the blunt tip of the handle to make holes and push the compost into place.

The most practical plants to choose are those which thrive in indirect light with lots of humidity, such as Delta maidenhair fern *Adiantum raddianum*, Moon Valley friendship plant *Pilea involucrata*, strawberry begonia *Saxifraga stolonifera*, button fern *Pellaea rotundifolia*, aluminium plant *Pilea cadierei* or polka dot plant *Hypoestes phyllostachya*. Try planting in groups of three, using the tallest as your main focal point and balancing it with a couple of other species of varying heights.

Avoid collecting plants from the wild, since they can harbour bacteria and disobedient insects, either of which can quickly take over your little piece of paradise in unexpected ways. A wide variety of terrarium plants can be found at most garden centres and specialist plant shops. Check their care requirements and select the ones that will work together. Remember not to overcrowd your terrarium as each plant will need space to grow.

Apply the same rules as any houseplant and keep light and humidity around the terrarium consistent, and steer clear of any areas in your home that may suddenly alter in temperature. If you notice a build-up of condensation, consider moving your terrarium to a cooler place with less direct light.

Since they are so easy to care for and require so little space, a terrarium is a great choice for a bedside table or work desk with little direct light – here it can inspire thoughts of faraway lands and be happy left to care for itself while you are on adventures in the wild outdoors.

GLASS VESSEL
TERRARIUM PLANTS
HOUSEPLANT COMPOST
GRAVEL
ACTIVATED CHARCOAL

WOODEN SPOON
DECORATION
GARDENING GLOVES

01

Put on gardening gloves, if you like. Begin with your base. Add around 2½cm/1in of gravel to the base of your vessel – this is for drainage and to encourage the circulation of moisture. Next, add a fine layer of activated charcoal, mixing it into the gravel. This will prevent stagnation and the growth of fungi.

02

Lay a bed of compost – the depth depends on the size of both your vessel and the plants. Generally speaking 5cm/2in is a good amount to start with if working with fairly small plants. Level the compost with your fingers and push it down gently to remove air pockets.

03

Using your fingers, make a hole in the terrarium compost at the point where you would like your first plant to sit. Taking the first plant out of its pot, gently loosen the compost around its roots and insert it into the hole. Holding it upright with one hand, press compost around it to hold it in place, making sure there are no air pockets around its roots.

04

At this stage you can use your wooden spoon to add more compost until the plant's roots are covered – only the stem and leaves should be exposed. Do this gently so as not to damage the roots. Once it is secure, repeat step 03 until all of your plants are in the chosen positions.

05

Clean around the inside of the glass using a clean cloth and carefully wipe plant leaves with some tissue or a soft brush if necessary. Water very lightly around the base of each plant with a misting bottle or pipette.

06

Add any decorations to embellish the scene, such as dried lichen, crystals and rocks. You can use stones to stabilise more delicate plants and little pieces of mirrored glass can add another dimension to your miniature world.

TERRARIUMS NEED LESS WATERING THAN A POTTED HOUSEPLANT,
BUT WATER IF THE SURFACE OF THE COMPOST FEELS DRY, OR USE YOUR
FINGERTIP TO CHECK THE MOISTURE IN THE COMPOST. IF PLANTS BEGIN TO
LOOK ROTTEN OR UNWELL, YOU CAN GENTLY REMOVE THEM AND REPLACE
WITH HEALTHY ONES. PRUNE ANY BROWN LEAVES TO IMPROVE THE
APPEARANCE OF THE PLANTS AND TRIM BACK ANY OVERGROWING STEMS.

NURTURING YOUR PLANTS

---

potting & repotting with homemade pots,
compost & fertiliser

There is something in the nature of plants that slows us down. Their primitive quality grounds us, and at the same time their intricacy demands focus, reminding us of the little details of life and our innate desire to nurture.

To watch another living thing flourish is rewarding, and we have come to see many of our plants as prickly pets, each with their own distinct personality. One miniature succulent might shower its bulbous leaves suggestively at the slightest nudge, while another will sit for years in cool suspense before one day bursting into bloom and making you drop your toast in alarm. It is this unique charm that makes plants a pleasure to live with, but knowing how to tend to each one can be a little daunting.

Once you have settled a plant in a place it can thrive, it will gradually begin to mature, purposely advancing into new spaces. In the case of a cactus, this will be towards the source of light. Other indoor plants, such as climbing vines, may produce aerial roots to support them as they seek out new territories to take hold of. At this point, you have the chance to influence a plant's growth, deciding whether to prune and maintain its size, or let it grow wild.

Whichever direction you choose, this chapter will give you practical advice on some of the basic ways you can encourage your plants to develop and stay healthy. Included are the essential ingredients and simple tools to get your hands dirty and keep your favourite plants blooming year after year, from choosing a suitable container and making your own organic compost, to learning how to cast your own lightweight concrete and coir pot.

CHOOSING
A CONTAINER

Although practical, the standard plastic pot (which your plant will most likely come in) is far from inspiring. Even a casual search for a more interesting container should uncover a huge variety of designs either to sit your plastic pot in, or to repot your characterful companion.

When styling a group of plants together, we choose pots of varied colours, shapes and textures, giving each plant its own unique look. Most basic containers can be bought at homeware shops or at your local garden centre. But if you are on the hunt for something more special, you can find some interesting and reasonably priced alternatives at charity shops, flea markets and antique fairs.

If you plan to discard your plant's plastic pot and repot directly into a new container, the main characteristic to consider is a drainage hole. This allows excess water to drain through the soil and be released – without a drainage hole, a plant's roots can become waterlogged and rotten. Additionally, consider the material of a container, which can also have an impact on the health of a plant (more on that below). If you do happen to fall in love with a pot without a drainage hole, you can simply place the original pot within it on top of a layer of gravel so that your plant's roots never sit in water.

PLASTIC

Easy to obtain and inexpensive, these reliable pots retain moisture for a long time while having adequate drainage holes at their base to allow the free flow of water. They also come in a variety of different sizes, which is helpful when you are repotting and need to step up to a pot that is only slightly larger than the original. Beware, though, as they can be flimsy and unsuitable for supporting larger, heavier plants.

UNGLAZED TERRACOTTA

Humble but reliable, the traditional terracotta pot has remained a favourite with the modern indoor gardener due to its versatility. Its porous nature makes it the perfect match for cacti and other succulents, allowing moisture to be absorbed and then any excess to evaporate. Terracotta also facilitates the free movement of oxygen around the roots of a plant, which aids their development and reduces the chance of rot.

These pots can become very heavy when wet and can be difficult to clean, but are useful for larger plants that need a solid base to keep them upright. Before repotting, soak new terracotta pots overnight in fresh water to stop them drawing too much water from their new inhabitant's soil.

CACHEPOT

This is the term given to a pot without a drainage hole that conceals a plant's original pot rather than replaces it. Pick a cachepot which is only a few centimetres/inches bigger than the original so that the plant doesn't appear overwhelmed. You can pick any design you like the look of, from unusual pottery to antique copper bowls. Just make sure the cachepot is waterproof, and tip out any excess water a few hours after each watering to avoid the roots sitting in a puddle.

RHIZOPOT

We recently began using these breathable pots for our indoor plants. Unlike plastic or ceramic pots, which can limit a plant's root function once they begin to circle around the edge, these innovative pots encourage roots to continue growing through the pot's walls. External dry air and light then stops them growing and encourages secondary roots within the soil to develop. This natural 'root pruning' prevents the roots circling around the edges of the pot and concentrates the root growth inside the pot where they will perform better. Rather than having to remove and replace the pot, a smaller RhizoPot can be planted directly into a larger RhizoPot, at which point the plant's outside roots will continue growing. This makes them particularly useful for propagation projects, when a young plant's roots are very fragile and vulnerable to damage from being disturbed.

Biodegradable and made from recycled materials, these pots need to be placed on a saucer, with excess water draining from their base as normal. Their porous nature means soil can dry out quickly, so be sure to keep on top of your watering routine.

SELF-WATERING PLANTER

Although not suitable for every plant, these innovative designs appeal to the low-maintenance indoor gardener who cannot tend to their plants on a regular basis, or who perhaps lacks a friendly neighbour to rely on while on holiday. Pot up with tropical plants that like high humidity and that like growing in consistently moist conditions. Lightweight in design, these pots are easy to clean, but are really function over form.

POT CLEANING | *Secondhand or pre-used pots should be cleaned in between plantings to get rid of infection and diseases. Soak each pot in a solution of 1 part vinegar, 3 parts water for 30 minutes, then rinse thoroughly. If the pot is made from porous terracotta, leave to soak until you are ready to repot to help conserve the compost's moisture.*

NO-MESS COIR AND CONCRETE POT

When you invest in a new plant for your home, it is not always easy to find a pot that stands up to the plant's unique personality. Whether metal, wood, ceramic or concrete, we have found the relationship between organic and man-made processes a huge inspiration. The delicacy of a flourishing plant contrasting with the robust, brutalist nature of a handmade concrete pot creates a wonderful sense of balance, and is a project that anyone can try at home with a few key ingredients.

Our lightweight coir and concrete pots were the result of one of Rose's early experiments. She was playing with different concrete blends that had to be strong, but not too heavy to put people off buying them from our market stall. By blending different aggregates with the cement she found that, although the pots took longer to cure and dry, they were lighter and had much more personality.

A good friend recommended we try using coir – a fibre extracted from the husk of coconuts – as an alternative to peat moss, which is often used in lighter concrete pot blends and is environmentally unsound to harvest. The coir produces a beautiful flecked grain after polishing, and, along with the vermiculite in the recipe, gives a wonderful texture and surprisingly lightweight finish.

This basic recipe will make a lightweight pot suitable for small or large moulds and will take a little longer to cure than a standard concrete pot, but is just as resilient.

Start by choosing inner and outer moulds of a similar shape, but which are a couple of centimetres/inches different in size – this will allow for an even wall. For as little mess as possible, choose a plastic outer mould with a lid so that you can combine the ingredients simply by popping the lid on and shaking. Avoid using any outer or inner moulds made from metal, glass or very rigid plastic, or those with a lipped edge, which can be difficult to release after the curing process.

If you plan to plant directly in the pot, you can use a drill to make a small drainage hole at its base after the pot has fully cured. Give your pot a good rinse afterwards to remove any excess dust. Otherwise, keep your plant in its plastic pot and simply sit it within the concrete pot to allow for drainage after watering.

If you are not able to do this project outdoors, find a well-ventilated space which is suitable for any accidental spillages, and wear gloves during all the steps. Before you begin, make sure you have a level area clear to leave your pot to cure, or you may end up with a wonky finish. Unless you like a wonky finish, of course.

OUTER AND INNER MOULD
GLOVES & DUST MASK
SPOON
RAGS OR TEA TOWEL
SMALL STONES OR SAND
PLASTIC BAG
SCALPEL OR SHARP KNIFE

1 PART GREY OR WHITE PORTLAND CEMENT
1 PART VERMICULITE OR PERLITE
1 PART COIR
1–1½ PARTS WATER

01

Put on your dust mask and gloves. Mix together equal parts cement, vermiculite and coir in your outer mould – use enough to fill it halfway full. If your outer mould has a lid, you can simply secure it and shake the ingredients together, keeping one hand firmly on the lid. Otherwise, use a spoon to mix the ingredients until they are evenly blended.

02

Add about two-thirds of the water to your mix and shake well, making sure the lid is secure at all times, or stir. Keep adding the remaining water until the mixture is like cottage cheese in consistency. Discard any of the water that remains.

03

Fill the inner mould with your small stones or sand to help it keep its shape. Push the central mould into the mix to form the inner hole of your pot. If the mixture reaches the very top of the inner mould, remove a little until there is at least 2cm/¾in free at the top. Line up the central mould so it is level with the top of the outer mould. You can now remove your mask.

04

Before leaving to cure, you can remove air bubbles by tapping the base of the mould on a surface to produce a smooth outer finish, or don't tap it if you would like to encourage irregular air holes and imperfections on the surface of your pot. Then encase your pot with a plastic bag and leave to cure for 48 hours. After curing, remove the pot from the bag and touch its rim: it should feel firm, but still very slightly damp. If it feels crumbly at this stage, return it to the bag and allow it to cure for a few hours longer.

05

Once set, tip out the stones or sand and remove the inner mould by either squeezing or cutting the rim and then pulling it out with a little force. To remove the concrete pot from the outer mould, turn both upside down and use the weight of your palm or even the heel of your foot to release it, or carefully cut the plastic away with a knife or scalpel.

06

Place the pot on a rag or towel and leave to fully cure on a non-absorbent surface for two weeks.

ONCE CURED, TRY LIGHTLY POLISHING THE OUTSIDE OF THE POT WITH SANDPAPER TO REVEAL SOME OF THE DETAIL OF THE INGREDIENTS WITHIN THE MIX.

REPOTTING

Plants and growth should go hand in hand. And although a plant will tolerate being kept in the same pot for some time, its health and vibrancy will slowly decline if the space allowed for its roots continues to be reduced. Roots are essential for the growth and health of your plant: they serve as an anchor to the main body of the plant, as well as helping to deliver water and nutrients to the plant's stems. Sticking with a small container is guaranteed to limit the future progression of your plant, since roots simply run out of available space. To solve this, it is best to repot – a process that is sometimes called 'potting up' or 'potting on' and involves transplanting a young plant into a proper container for the first time, or moving one from an existing container into a bigger one. By giving them greater freedom to roam and the opportunity to seek out more nutrients and water, you can actively encourage root development so that your plants can grow faster and stronger, and will appear more vibrant and healthy.

To identify when a plant needs to be repotted, look out for external signifiers of crowded space, such as roots coming through the pot's drainage holes, a bulging pot or the plant's languishing health. In order to know for definite when it is time to move a plant on to a larger pot, you have to get a bit closer and check the roots themselves.

The method of checking a plant's roots depends on the kind of plant. For a tropical plant or leafy succulent, carefully support the base of the plant between your fingers where its stems meet the soil (just spread your fingers and rest the palm of your hand on the surface of the soil). Then tip the pot upside down and remove the plant, tapping the base of the pot gently if it doesn't come away easily. In the search to replenish their source of growth, overgrown roots will begin to circle, cluster and form a mass at the base of the pot: this is when a plant becomes 'pot bound' and its roots become most vulnerable to changes in moisture and temperature. Apart from a few varieties, such as the urn plant (which hates to be repotted), most will suffer if they are allowed to remain in this state.

To check whether a cactus needs to be repotted, use the method above, but you may need a pair of thick gloves or some scrunched-up newspaper to protect your hands and the plant. If the plant does not come away easily from the pot, poke a pencil through the pot's drainage holes to loosen the soil. Alternatively, if plastic, give the pot a gentle squeeze, which will often release the plant with little force. If the roots are not yet visible and the compost looks fairly loose and fresh, carefully replace the pot and continue to care for it as usual. If the roots are clearly visible, or have formed a white mass at the base of the pot, with little soil visible, it is time to repot.

A NOTE ON TOPDRESSING | *For large potted plants or more delicate varieties that do not like to be disturbed, the top layer of potting mixture can be removed and replaced with fresh compost each spring, replenishing the plant with nutrients without causing it distress.*

Nurturing Your Plants

The prime time to repot any houseplants is in early spring, when they are moving into their active growth period. At this active stage, their roots are better able to absorb water and nutrients and they can avoid a build-up of moisture which causes rot. Repotting is a good way to remove old, nutrient-lacking soil and replenish your plant with fresh nutrients to promote new growth.

Before you repot your plant, think about which container you want to use and make sure you clean it thoroughly (see p75–76 for advice on choosing the right pot and getting it ready). To ensure the optimum health of your plant, water needs to be able to pass freely through the container, so be sure to pick one with at least one drainage hole in its base. Plants will sit and sulk when moved into a pot much bigger than their original, since surplus compost may become waterlogged and cause a plant's roots to suffer. So be kind and choose a pot that gives only an extra 2–4cm/1–2in diameter around the existing roots.

01   Remove the plant from its pot and check its compost for signs of pests or rot. Areas of rot and compacted compost should be carefully removed and discarded – take care not to damage the roots. Gently massage the compost, shaking away any excess soil and teasing the roots to loosen them. Lay the plant on its side on a clear surface, taking care not to bend its leaves.

02   If your new pot has a single drainage hole, place a piece of broken pottery, gauze or newspaper in the base to stop the new compost running straight through once you begin watering. A plastic pot with lots of holes does not need a drainage layer, so you can pot straight in.

03   Add in a layer of your potting medium (your can make your own with our recipes on p91, or use your favourite shop-bought general houseplant mix). Add enough so that the plant sits comfortably, the base of its stems and the soil level 2cm/¾in from the top rim.

04   Place your plant gently inside the pot. Using a spoon or small trowel, add the new potting medium evenly around the edges of the roots until the plant is well supported, leaving 2cm/¾in of free space at the top to allow for watering. You can tap the edges of the pot gently to ensure the compost is evenly settled, but there is no need to pack it in too firmly.

05   Finally, water the plant from its base by sitting it in a bowl of water. Allow it to absorb enough so that the top of the compost feels moist, then remove it from the water and allow to drain. With tropical plants, choose a shady area away from any direct light for its first week in a new pot while it acclimatises to its new environment. Mist its leaves daily if it shows signs of wilting. For cacti and other succulents, do not water the plant again for 1–2 weeks, or a little longer if you think the roots were damaged during the repotting process.

POTTING
MEDIUMS

Picking the right potting medium to nurture each of your indoor plants is key. Since pH levels and drainage all play an important role in the health of different species, the medium must contain essential nutrients, preserve the right amount of moisture and be loose enough to allow for the movement of water, oxygen and healthy root growth.

For most foliage houseplants, an all-purpose houseplant compost is suitable, but these often have added fertilisers and moisture-retaining ingredients that will not provide suitable conditions for cacti and other succulents as they don't mimic these plants' natural habitats. Cacti compost can be bought from most garden specialists, and are often blended with ingredients such as sand to help with drainage.

However, many shop-bought composts of all varieties contain an ingredient called peat moss, and this is something we avoid using and would not encourage people to plant in. Peat comes from the decomposed remains of a species of moss called sphagnum moss. It is mined from bogs, has no nutrient value, and is not a renewable resource since it takes centuries to develop. The best substitute we have found for peat is coir: it is a fibre extracted from the husk of coconuts and it is what we happily use as a base in all our potting mixtures. We started making our own mixes as a cheaper and more sustainable alternative to peat-based products. On p91 we have shared these simple recipes and each of the plants featured in the House of Plants chapter on p123 includes a note on the most suitable compost.

To feed your plants extra goodness, you can also enhance the compost with various products. During the spring, we often use a product called Charge by Ecothrive. It is made entirely from the droppings of organically reared beetles – what better way to show your plants you love them than with beetle poo? – and is approved by the Soil Association for use in organic growing. You can sprinkle it on the top of your compost every couple of months and it is gradually absorbed every time you water your plants. Liquid fertilisers are also a good option: these are quickly absorbed by the plant, providing a fast hit of nutrients. Our favourites are made from natural sources such as comfrey, nettles or seaweed, which you can buy premade, or see p95 for our homemade fertiliser.

REPOTTING AFTERCARE | *If a plant's old potting mix looks very different to the new compost, keep an eye on the moisture level of any remaining older soil around the base of the plant's central stems. It may need watering more than the surrounding compost while the plant's roots settle and begin to spread out – to do this, simply water directly onto the older soil.*

Nurturing Your Plants

HOMEMADE COMPOST RECIPES

01

TROPICAL HOUSEPLANT COMPOST

This medium is suitable for all of the tropical plants featured in this book. As a base, the coir works by retaining moisture, allowing the plant's roots to absorb as much as it needs. Rock dust and worm castings contain essential minerals, each adding long-lasting nutrients to the compost, enriching the plant's health.

INGREDIENTS

8 PARTS COIR
2 PARTS WORM CASTINGS
A PINCH OF ROCK DUST
A SPRINKLE OF ECOTHRIVE
CHARGE

TIP

FOR PROPAGATING TROPICAL
PLANTS, REDUCE WORM
CASTINGS TO 1 PART

02

CACTI & OTHER SUCCULENTS COMPOST

This simple mixture encourages effective drainage, with the coarse sand, grit or perlite allowing water to pass through the compost quickly to prevent root rot. It is also suitable for propagating cactus offsets. We find a cup is a handy measuring tool.

MATERIALS

1 PART COIR
1 PART HORTICULTURAL
COARSE SAND, 3-4MM/^{1}/₈IN
HORTICULTURAL GRIT OR PERLITE

TIP

THE BRITISH CACTI AND
SUCCULENT SOCIETY
RECOMMEND CAT LITTER AS
A CHEAPER ALTERNATIVE TO
PERLITE – BUT BE SURE TO
PICK A VARIETY THAT IS DUST
FREE AND NON-CLUMPING

HOMEBREW NETTLE FERTILISER

There's nothing like a flourishing houseplant to spur you along on your indoor gardening journey – and a little natural fertiliser (either solid or liquid) can really encourage plants to thrive and flower during their active growth period. Many people choose not to bother with these supplements, which is fine in the short term, but if you do decide to bestow on your plants a little extra love and attention, you will soon be rewarded with very happy, healthy bloomers.

Most commercial, multi-purpose composts contain roughly enough fertiliser to adequately feed a plant for six weeks. Therefore it is a good idea to begin feeding a plant around six weeks after repotting. The frequency of feeding will depend on the kind of plant: each plant focus page in our House of Plants chapter (p123) will tell you how often is necessary. Don't be tempted to try and over-fertilise your plants – they will rebel! Cacti and succulents in particular hate being over-nourished, and respond to your extra enthusiasm by becoming unhealthily soft, fleshy and prone to infections.

This project will show you how to make your own liquid fertiliser using nettles – a common weed, easily found. Although people see them as a nuisance, nettles often grow in areas where the soil is high in nitrogen, absorbing it as they develop along with many other minerals. Used as a fertiliser, these nutrient-rich weeds are a great source of nourishment to other plants, feeding their roots with minerals such as nitrogen, iron, zinc and many essential trace elements.

TOOLS AND MATERIALS

FRESHLY CUT NETTLES
RAINWATER OR OTHER NON-CHLORINATED WATER
GLOVES
BUCKET
WEIGHT (SUCH AS A BRICK)
STORAGE JARS

01

First, pick your nettles. Harvest roughly enough to line the base of your bucket (the bigger the bucket, the more fertiliser you will make). Young stems are best, since they will break up more easily. Make sure to wear thick protective gloves as nettles will irritate the skin.

02

Scrunch and tear up the stems and leaves with your gloved hands and layer them at the bottom of the bucket, packing them down firmly. This step will thoroughly bruise the nettles and cause them to break down as quickly as possible.

03

Lay your weight on top of the crushed nettles to hold them firmly in place at the bottom of the bucket. You can use any heavy material you can find for this, such as a brick, slab of stone or separate container filled with stones.

04

Fill the bucket with water so that the nettles are completely covered. Leave enough space below the rim of the bucket to allow for a bit of foam as the tonic ferments. Place the bucket somewhere sheltered outside, but in indirect light. Check its progress every couple of weeks and give it an occasional stir. Be aware that the tonic becomes very pungent as the nettles break down, so keep it well away from your house if possible.

05

Once the liquid stops bubbling (after a month or so), it is ready to be used. Pour the nutrient-rich liquid from the bucket into a fresh container, using a strainer if you like. The nettles remaining in the bucket can be discarded, or can be topped up with fresh nettles and re-covered with the weight and water if you would like to continue brewing more tonic.

06

To make the final fertiliser, dilute the brewed liquid: one part nettle liquid to ten parts fresh water. Store the fertiliser in a cool, dark place. Always make up your final fertiliser straight away as the brewed nettle liquid smells rather powerful when left neat. Use the fertiliser in the spring and summer to nourish your indoor plants – simply pour a little into their watering trays. The quantity produced should last you the whole season.

IF YOU WOULD LIKE TO TRY MAKING DIFFERENT LIQUID FERTILISERS,
ALTERNATIVES TO NETTLES INCLUDE THE WIDELY USED COMFREY,
BRACKEN LEAVES, CHICORY, CLOVER AND STRAWBERRY LEAVES.
ALL CAN BE PICKED IN THE SPRING OR SUMMER.

Nurturing Your Plants

SHARING YOUR PLANTS

cuttings, division & offsets

We all have our favourite indoor plant. It is the one we inherited, or one that survived a long journey; it's that capricious cactus, or perhaps the plant that we rescued and revived. The incredible thing is that with a little patience and at almost no cost, it is extremely easy to propagate most houseplants and start producing new, very familiar siblings.

Propagation is also an inspiring way to explain the wonders of botany to children, showing them how satisfying it can be to grow their own plant that they can nurture and treasure, and perhaps go on to share with their friends. The tools and materials needed for most methods are minimal and inexpensive and can be reused if any experiments are unsuccessful.

For us, sharing our favourite plants is also a way of reducing needless waste by being resourceful and valuing the things we consider precious. Once you have practised the following propagation techniques, you can begin to cultivate and share a new generation of your favourite plants, gradually multiplying your stock (without having to go shopping) and enjoying a bit of creative experimentation in a completely sustainable way.

There are various methods of propagation, both sexual and asexual, that work with certain families of plants. Cacti, for example, can be grown from seed, divided at the roots or grafted from the tip of a parent plant. However, most popular houseplants will not produce seeds indoors, since they are unlikely to be pollinated away from their natural habitat. In this chapter we have included the methods that we have found to be the fastest and most successful.

PROPAGATION

Propagation is the method of producing new plants from existing ones. Its most obvious benefit is that it allows you to increase your collection and share new plants. But propagation can also be a useful next step after you've pruned a more mature plant; or you may find that a favourite plant becomes unwell in its old age and by propagating a part of it that is still healthy, you can replicate its charm with a brand new specimen.

Whatever your reason for propagation, there are various methods that work successfully for different cacti, succulents and tropical plants. The fastest methods involve using a part of a parent plant such as a stem, leaf or offset. This is called asexual or 'vegetative' propagation and does not require pollination. Many succulents, particularly sedums, are keen to shed their leaves with little encouragement and these are the prime candidates for leaf propagation.

Most species of plants can be grown from seeds (or spores, in the case of ferns and mosses), but when kept indoors are very unlikely to be pollinated. Shop-bought seeds can be experimented with, but they are notoriously difficult to germinate without proper equipment to regulate temperate and humidity. Therefore, we have focused on vegetative propagation in this chapter, the avocado seed propagation being the only exception. If you would like to experiment with other kinds of seed propagation, try starting with cacti, ficus and bromeliad seeds.

The ideal time to propagate is in a plant's active growth period, typically in spring and summer months. We advise feeding the parent plant with an organic fertiliser (such as our homemade nettle fertiliser on p95) a few months or weeks before you propagate, ensuring it is as healthy and resilient as possible. This is not essential, though, and most methods will work well without any use of fertiliser or supplements.

Before attempting to propagate with any of the following techniques, do a little research to check if your plant is suitable for the method you would like to try. Certain plants such as ferns, for example, will not grow from a stem cutting and must be either grown from spores or propagated by division. If you would like to propagate a plant that features in the House of Plants chapter on p123, check those pages first as we have included the best propagation method for each plant.

Air plants are not covered in this chapter, as they propagate by producing offsets that must remain attached to the parent plant until they become completely independent. More information on this can be found on p114.

LEAF

CUTTING

{ *echeveria* }

Many plants can be successfully propagated by removing whole or part of a parent plant's leaves. Similar in many ways to stem cuttings, propagation by leaf cutting can produce a vast amount of new stock, but requires a little more patience as it takes a while longer for each leaf to develop its own root system.

Fleshy-leaved succulents are made for this method as they naturally shed their lower leaves. In the case of many species of echeveria, crassula or sedum, you can remove healthy leaves still attached by gently plucking them – just make sure to remove the entire leaf down to the stem.

In the case of larger tropical plants such as the snake plant (p183) and some species of pilea, you only need to cut the top section of the leaf in order for it to root when placed in the rooting medium. As a container, you can use any shallow tray or dish which will comfortably allow around 3cm/1½in of rooting medium.

You can also use this method to 'recycle' a plant that has become leggy and less attractive due to insufficient light or old age. Species of echeveria and sedum often become quite stalky as they develop, especially if they haven't received enough light. If this happens, you can simply remove all of the plant's healthy leaves and produce lots of new, replica plants by following the steps on p104. Or if the top of the plant is still attractive, you can simply cut the top section off and treat it as a stem cutting (see p106).

PLANNING | *Remember that your propagated leaves will eventually require similar conditions to those of the parent plant. If you are using this method to propagate a sun-loving succulent, for example, consider that you will need enough space with direct light for them all to bask.*

Sharing Your Plants

01	To make a rooting medium, mix two parts cactus compost to one part sand (or use our homemade compost recipe number 02 on p91). Make enough medium to fill your rooting tray to a depth of around 3cm/1½in. Pack the medium down gently and spray the entire surface with enough water to make it feel damp to the touch.
02	Using your fingers, remove each leaf from the parent plant where it meets the stem. Select leaves that look healthy; avoid any that may be wilting or discoloured. For echeveria, crassula and other fleshy-leaved plants, leave each detached leaf a couple of days (somewhere warm and away from direct light) to callus over. This is to prevent rot from forming. For tropical plants, you can continue to step 03 without waiting.
03	When ready, lay each leaf onto the rooting medium and ensure that the raw edge of the leaf is at least partly touching the surface. If propagating a tropical plant such as a snake plant (p183), you may need to insert the raw edge of the leaf cutting into the compost so the leaves sit upright to ensure root growth. Pick a spot for the rooting tray where it will be warm and will receive indirect light. It does not need to be covered, but regularly check that the medium is slightly moist with your finger, being careful not to disturb any of the developing leaves. If it has dried out, you can carefully mist the surface with a little water.
04	After a month or so, you should see the start of roots forming. In another month, a tiny rosette of leaves will begin to take shape. Once the roots are long enough, cover them with a little of the soil to encourage their growth.
05	When the new roots have settled into the soil, use your hands or a spoon to gently remove the baby plant together with the soil around it, and repot it into a small container filled with a cactus compost.

STEM
CUTTING

{ *Chinese money plant* }

Taking stem cuttings from your plants is one of the fastest ways to increase your stock. It requires little space and is a successful method for many families of popular plants, from tropical foliage species to fleshy succulents. As well as producing new replicas of your favourites at little cost, this method is also beneficial to the parent plant. By pruning more mature stems in order to propagate, you can reshape the original plant and encourage its younger stems to grow stronger.

Plants featured in this book which can successfully be propagated by stem cuttings include the golden pothos (p127), Chinese money plant (p133), monstera (p147) and jade plant (p153). Other suitable plants include dracaena, euphorbia, citrus, coffee and many succulent species. Make sure to water the parent plant the day before you take cuttings to ensure its stems are not too dry when they are cut.

Prepare the rooting container before you begin to prevent the cuttings drying out during the steps on p108. To regulate the temperature and humidity, a sealed container should be used until the cuttings take root. You can either buy a shop-bought rooting container or create your own by cutting the top off a few plastic bottles and placing them over the top of each cutting. Alternatively, you can encase the container inside a plastic bag. To prevent moisture loss, use a fairly large, shallow base made from a non-porous material such as plastic or metal. It should have drainage holes so that excess water can escape, or a layer of drainage stones or gravel if no drainage holes are present.

POST-PROPAGATION | *To repot each cutting, choose a container which allows roughly 5cm/2in of space around the edge of the roots. You can use our compost recipe 01 on p91, reducing worm castings to 1 part. Alternatively, you can use a peat-free seedling compost.*

Sharing Your Plants

01   First mix equal parts coir (or general houseplant compost) and perlite (or vermiculite). Make enough to fill your rooting container to a depth of around 5cm/2in. Pack the medium down gently and spray the entire surface with enough water to make it feel moist to the touch.

02   To take a stem cutting, make a cut around 5cm/2in below the point where a leaf and stem meet with a clean knife or sharp pair of scissors. This will prevent crushing the stem tissue, which can make the plant vulnerable to disease. Choose a mature stem of the plant to cut, ideally with at least three nodes (where leaves meet the stem). Once cut, you can gently pull off smaller leaves lower down to encourage nutrients in the medium to nourish new roots.

03   Carry out the next step quickly to make sure the tip of the cutting remains as moist as possible. Insert the raw end of each stem cutting into the rooting medium, just deep enough to support it. Make sure there is enough room below the buried section to allow for new roots to form. Space the cuttings out so each has enough room to take root.

04   Water or mist the cuttings, seal the container to increase warmth and humidity. Place the container somewhere 23–28°C / 73–82°F, where it will receive plenty of indirect light.

05   Leave the cuttings for between three weeks to two months. Throughout the rooting process, test the moisture level of the soil by gently inserting your finger at the edge of the tray – be careful not to knock any of the cuttings. The soil should feel damp, but water should never collect in the impression left by your finger. If the soil is too wet, leave it for a few days or until it has dried out slightly. If the soil is too dry, mist it until it is damp all over.

06   After a minimum of three weeks, gently try to remove one of the cuttings from the medium to check for new roots. If you find there is no resistance and little or no roots have formed, return the cutting and press the medium back around its base to secure it in place. There should be some resistance and roots should be around 4cm/1¾in long before transplanting the cutting to a new pot.

07   Once the cuttings are ready to be repotted, allow them to adjust to your home environment. Open the container for an hour or so on the first day before resealing, then gradually allow longer exposure the following days to help the cutting acclimatise. If the leaves of the cuttings start to wilt, slow this process down. Once the cuttings are able to be removed from the container without wilting, they should be ready to repot.

Sharing Your Plants

DIVISION

{ jade }

For plants that grow in clusters or have separate stems (such as yucca, calathea, fern and some succulent species), the easiest method of propagation is division. With this process, the whole plant is cut into sections allowing each part to continue to develop and grow, often with more strength than if it was left whole. This method is the best way to keep fast-growing succulents such as the jade plant at a preferred size – as a pleasing bonus, you will be producing new plants to fill vacant spaces or to give to lucky friends.

Plants featured in this book suitable for division include the cast iron plant (p130), oxalis (p144) and snake plant (p183). However, due to their root systems, not all stemmed species of plants can be successfully divided in this way, so do a little research before you get your knife out.

You can use this method to reduce the size of a parent plant very subtly (by separating off only a small section) or you can separate the parent plant into as many new parts as it will divide into. It really depends on how many new plants you wish to produce.

Before you begin, prepare the pots you would like to replant your divided plant into. Choose pots that are a little larger than the divided parts, giving enough room (about 5cm/2in) for new roots to develop. Put a layer of drainage stones in the base of each pot.

This method of propagation is probably the messiest, so find a location in your home or outside that you can scatter in soil. We normally work over a large tablecloth on a free surface to catch all the rogue soil, which can easily be flung into the garden afterwards.

01   First make sure you have a good mound of potting medium to hand. We recommend using one of our compost recipes on p91, or use a commercial houseplant compost. The amount you need will depend on the number of divided parts being propagated and the number of pots you wish to plant them in.

02   Carefully remove the plant to be propagated from its pot. For tropical plants and succulents, the easiest way to do this is by resting the palm of your hand flat along the surface of the soil, supporting the plant's stems, and turning the pot upside down. If you need more guidance, see p84.

03   Return the plant to its upright position and gently massage the soil to determine how easily its roots will separate. Do not worry if you lose most of the original potting mixture. If your plant has delicate roots, only massage the soil away until the plant has separated. If your plant has thicker roots, continue to massage to remove as much old compost as you can, allowing nutrient-rich fresh compost to be used in the next step. If the root system is very tangled or rigid, you can use a sharp knife to slice through the clusters of soil. However, this should be avoided if possible, as it will inevitably damage the more delicate roots. Once finished, lay each new section of plant on your work surface.

04   You can now repot each section. Put a little of your potting medium in the base of each pot, leaving enough space for the new plants to sit comfortably. Hold the new plant inside its allocated pot, and with your other hand or a trowel add enough mixture to fill all the gaps around its sides. You can gently tap the base of the pot on a hard surface to distribute the compost evenly.

05   Once the pot is full of potting medium and the plant is upright and supported stably, press down firmly on the soil around the base of the plant's stems. This will remove any little air pockets that might still be present.

POST-PROPAGATION | *Place each new plant in similar conditions to the parent plant's original conditions. With tropical plants in particular, if any of the divided plants begins to wilt, encase it in a plastic bag to increase humidity until it looks healthy again.*

OFFSETS

{ Easter lily cactus }

Many plants regularly produce offsets – they are miniature replicas of the parent plant that normally grow around the stem. Depending on the family, offsets can appear around the base of the plant's stem or much higher up. Plants that often produce offsets include many desert cacti, bromeliad, banana, palm and agave species.

It is wonderful when it happens as you are gifted with many more beautiful plants. But it is important not to be too keen in propagating, as these offsets should never be removed until they have developed enough to live independently. Judging when an offset is ready to be removed will depend on the plant type, but with desert cacti, we advise waiting until the offset is at least 3–5cm/1–2in long.

It is best to propagate in the spring or summer, when plants are entering their active growth period. And make sure you have their new home ready: like all propagated plants, each offset will require similar living conditions to the parent plant.

PROPAGATING AIR PLANTS | *After flowering, your air plant may produce one or more offsets, commonly called 'pups', between its leaves. These are mini replicas of the parent plant, and can be left attached to grow as one connected bunch, or removed to produce new independently living air plants. Try to resist removing these new plants until they are able to survive without the support of the parent plant: this is once they have reached at least a third of the size of the parent plant. At this point, give the parent air plant a good soaking, and then remove the offsets by pulling them gently downwards.*

01   Use tongs or wear gardening gloves during the following steps to protect your fingers from any stray spines. A piece of scrunched-up newspaper will also help to keep a cactus steady while you are handling it.

02   If the offset is growing at the base of the parent plant and already has roots, use tongs or your fingers to gently ease it away from the main stem. If no roots are present, or if the roots seem too rigid to separate, use a knife to carefully cut away the offset. Make sure that you use a clean, sharp knife to prevent any damage to both parent plant and offset.

03   Once you have removed the offset, leave it on a clean surface away from direct light to allow the cut end to dry and seal over. This is to stop bacteria damaging the new plant. It may take anywhere between a couple of days and a week. Once the cut end is completely dry, it is ready to be planted.

04   The rooting medium you use will depend on whether the offset has roots or not. For offsets with no roots, use equal parts coir and sharp sand. For offsets which already have roots, mix equal parts potting compost recipe 02 (p91) or peat-free commercial cactus compost to sharp sand. Allow enough medium to fill your rooting container to a depth of around 3cm/1½in. Pack the medium down gently, and spray the surface with a little water, just enough to make it feel damp to the touch.

05   Make a shallow hole in the rooting medium and insert the offset. If there are no roots present, the offset only needs to be deep enough to hold it steady. If roots are present, cover them in the medium, pressing down gently to hold them secure.

Leave the offsets where they will receive light until the following spring, when they can be repotted.

SEEDS

{ *Avocado* }

The next time you enjoy an avocado, mango or lychee, rather than throwing away the pit (seed), try growing your own, fruity indoor plant. Although it is unlikely they will produce fruit (unless allowed to mature outdoors in warm climates), this method of propagation costs nothing and is a great project to try out with children – they will learn a lot about the basics of germination.

Native to Central and South America, avocado plants love to bathe in lots of bright light, so make sure you have a sunny home for the plant once it starts to sprout. Many other plants such as cacti, succulents and most tropical plants can be grown from seed, but the process is much more technical and time-consuming. Since very few plants produce seeds when kept indoors away from their natural habitat, the easiest way to experiment is by sourcing seeds from a gardening store or online.

01   Once you have removed the pit from the avocado, wash any leftover flesh by rinsing it under the tap. Take care not to damage the surface of the pit itself. The slightly pointed end is where the new shoot will grow, and the fatter bottom is where roots will develop.

02   Holding the narrowest point of the pit towards the ceiling, carefully pierce around the edge with three or four cocktail sticks or skewers (about 2cm/¾in deep) to hold it steady. The sticks will act as props to hold the pit partially submerged in water.

03   Fill a glass with water and balance the pit, fattest end facing downwards, on the rim of the glass. Make sure there is enough water in the glass to keep the base of the pip submerged. You will need to refresh the water every couple of days to prevent mould growing.

04   Place the glass somewhere with bright light. After a few weeks, the pit will start to split open and sprout new roots in the water. A couple of weeks later, you should begin to see shoots emerging from the top. It is important that the roots are kept submerged in water at all times.

05   Once the new avocado plant is around 20cm/8in tall, you can transfer it to a pot, planting it in compost and leaving the top of the pit exposed. The soil should be consistently moist, but never saturated with water.

Sharing Your Plants

HOUSE
OF PLANTS

---

the perfect plant for the perfect spot

We have enjoyed many moments of amused wonder while researching this book. Best were the serious instructions given by 1970s interior plant styling books, encouraging sensible consideration of greenery that 'bonded well' with existing furnishings, strict warnings against clashing leaf patterns and the faux pas of asymmetric pruning. One awe-inspiring centrepiece suggestion – a towering composition of bracken, twigs and moss mounds – produced a howl of glee from Rose which reverberated around an otherwise silent reading room of the British Library.

Since each person's living conditions are so varied, this chapter focuses on practical spots relevant to most homes, rather than specific rooms. Each plant focus page includes the sort of information our customers ask us, such as how often to water, when to repot and the prime method of propagation. The information on light, temperature and humidity should help you decide how to transform a space with luscious bursts of greenery. We tried only to highlight factors that are integral to the plant's health, so you should refer to the Knowing Your Plants chapter (p19) for general advice on how to tend and water your plants. Finally, we have featured alternative plants that enjoy similar conditions, so that you can collect a selection of plants that fit a space.

Along the way, you will find inspiration rather than instruction, including many styling tips that we have found make the biggest impact, from little details such as mirrors, to more functional decorations like plant stands and hanging planters. We hope the following pages will inspire you to see the potential of the space you live in and create unexpected pockets of greenery in the place you call home.

THE PRIVATE WINDOW

{ trailing, hanging, hiding }

We cannot all enjoy views of rolling landscapes and open skies, particularly living in urban apartments where we often overlook each other's homes. Whether the aim is to hide an uninspiring outside view or to hide yourself from outside viewers, a trailing tropical plant will act as an exotic screen, instantly adding a little mystery to any exposed room.

Bedrooms and bathrooms tend to be fairly shady, so the key is to find a foliage plant that likes little direct sunlight. Trailing tropical genera such as philodendrons and scindapsus are good options, and an occasional pruning of their tips will encourage bushiness. Humidity-loving tropical plants such as the asparagus fern will naturally absorb moisture from the atmosphere and may require less frequent watering to keep healthy.

If it is not possible to hang your plants, free-standing tropical varieties such as the cast iron plant will frame a window with little support and will provide some privacy without blocking out too much light.

GOLDEN POTHOS

Devil's ivy | Scindapsus | Silver vine
Botanical Name *Epipremnum aureum*
Family Araceae
Native To Solomon Islands
Suggested Alternatives Heartleaf philodendron / English ivy

Delightfully difficult to kill, the golden pothos will survive in rooms with little natural light and is resilient to forgetful owners, happily reviving after missing a watering. It is unlikely to bloom indoors, but its distinctly marbled leaves provide beauty enough, whether climbing a supportive moss pole or delicately trailing from a hanging planter or bookshelf. A particularly speedy grower, the golden pothos is good at providing a bit of privacy in an overlooked bathroom or bedroom, and is also efficient at removing certain toxins found in paints and furnishings.

LIGHT	Growth will be slow if you choose a very dark corner – the plant will grow with sparse vines and leaves quite far apart. Very bright locations will eventually destroy the plant. Choose a place where your plant will receive indirect light
TEMPERATURE	In the range of 18°C–24°C / 65°F–75°F throughout the year, and no cooler than 10°C / 50°F in winter
WATERING	Keep the compost moist in spring and summer, reducing significantly in winter. It does not mind being underwatered, but avoid overwatering as it can lead to mould growth
FEEDING	Nourish with a fertiliser every two weeks
REPOTTING	When necessary, repot in the spring. Use potting compost number 01 (p91)
PROPAGATION	Propagate in spring with stem cuttings (p106)

REPOTTING | *The golden pothos will grow aerial roots if it requires extra support or nourishment – a clear sign that it is time to either repot or prune your plant.*

ASPARAGUS FERN

Feathery asparagus | Lace fern
Botanical Name *Asparagus setaceus*
Family Asparagaceae
Native To Southern and Eastern Africa
Suggested Alternatives Delta maidenhair fern / Boston fern / Staghorn fern

Masquerading as a fern and until very recently classified as a lily, the asparagus fern in fact belongs to neither of these families of plants. With its fine, feathery leaves, it works well in a stand-alone pot or in a hanging planter and will grow up to 90cm/35in tall if left unpruned. Suited to bathrooms with high humidity, it requires a weekly watering to keep its compost moist during spring and summer.

LIGHT	Choose a room with bright, filtered light and keep the plant away from direct sunlight, which can scorch its leaves
TEMPERATURE	In the range of 18°C–24°C / 65°F–75°F throughout the year, and no cooler than 10°C / 50°F in winter
WATERING	Keep the compost moist during spring and summer, but never saturated. In autumn and winter, water sparingly, but never allow the compost to dry out completely. Mist regularly for optimum health
FEEDING	Nourish with a fertiliser every 2 weeks from early spring to early autumn
REPOTTING	Repot annually in the spring. Sit the plant low in its pot and add an extra 2.5cm/1in layer of compost to allow tuberous roots to surface as they grow. Use potting compost number 02 (p91)
PROPAGATION	Propagate in spring by division (p111)

CULTIVATION | *Overgrown stems and dried, golden fronds can be trimmed to maintain your plant's silhouette. Mature stems become woody over time and develop sharp spines, so be careful when pruning and wear gloves.*

CAST IRON PLANT

Bar room plant | Haran plant
Botanical Name *Aspidistra elatior*
Family Asparagaceae
Native To Japan and Taiwan
Suggested Alternatives Dracaena / Parlour palm

A favourite among English Victorians – and named in honour of its tolerance to conditions of low light and temperature – the cast iron plant became a symbol of middle-class life, before eventually being deemed a little old-fashioned. With its deep green leaves and elegant stems, it has come back into favour again. It needs very little care and adds an understated touch of the tropics to any shady room, growing to a regal height of around 70cm/28in and featuring delicate leaves that gradually turn a deeper shade of green as they develop. Look out for the cream-striped variety, which is seductively attractive but less hardy.

LIGHT	Native to forest floors, it is best suited to a north-facing window (i.e. low-light), but will also survive in shady hallways and corners. Bright light will scorch its leaves
TEMPERATURE	Very forgiving, you can place the plant in warm or cold indoor temperatures
WATERING	Water when the top 3cm/1½in of soil feel completely dry. Overwatering is this plant's biggest killer. Good drainage is key to its health so make sure the plant's roots never become saturated with water – think about planting it in a terracotta pot with good drainage, remembering to empty its drainage tray a few hours after watering
FEEDING	Feed with a diluted liquid fertiliser once a month during spring and summer
REPOTTING	When necessary, repot in the spring – though you should really only need to do this every four years
PROPAGATION	Propagate in spring by division (p111)

CHINESE MONEY PLANT

Missionary plant
Botanical Name *Pilea peperomioides*
Family Urticaceae
Native To West Indies
Suggested Alternatives Aluminium plant / Watermelon peperomia

One of our absolute favourite windowsill plants, this lily pad-shaped pilea is easy to grow and requires no pruning. Its dark green leaves eventually flourish from a single stem and bloom in delicate white flowers come summer. *Pilea peperomioides* isn't the easiest species to track down, but once you do it is easily propagated by stem cuttings and makes a great gift for fellow plant-loving friends.

LIGHT	Choose a bright position, but avoid sitting it in direct sunlight, which can damage the plant's fleshy leaves
TEMPERATURE	In the range of 25°C / 77°F and no cooler than 12°C / 54°F in winter. But always keep the plant away from draughty windows
WATERING	This plant comes to life in rooms with high humidity. During its active growth period, keep its compost evenly moist, but allow it to dry out between each watering. Drainage is key, so make sure its roots never sit in water. Reduce watering in the winter
FEEDING	Feed every two weeks during spring and summer
REPOTTING	When necessary, repot in spring. Use houseplant compost 01 (p91)
PROPAGATION	Propagate by stem cuttings in early spring (p106)

CLEANING | *If dust settles on a mature plant's leaves, gently wipe each one with a clean, damp cloth to show off its shiny surface.*

MACRAMÉ HANGING PLANTER

Landlords do not always encourage creative DIY and often our customers living in rented properties tell us they would love a hanging planter or two, but are unsure about hanging them without damaging the walls. With a little bit of creativity and a few simple materials, it is easier than expected to make the most of hanging space which might otherwise go unnoticed. If you are unable to hammer a nail or hook into the ceiling or wall, try suspending your planter from a curtain pole, coat hook or an S-hook hanging over the edge of a wardrobe, shelf or kitchen cupboard. Wherever you choose to hang your planter, just look out for a spot that matches the light requirements of your displayed plants.

This hanging planter design is a simple take on the retro macramé planters of the 1970s and only takes ten minutes or so to make. Once you have started with the basics, you can embellish the design with endless options of macramé knots, beads, metal rings or other accessories.

You can choose any rope you like: some of the most successful options we have experimented with include braided cotton, hemp and jute, which are inexpensive and strong enough to hold a fairly heavy plant.

To make watering as easy as possible, you can add a drainage tray below the plant pot so that you never have to remove it from the hanger.

01

Cut your rope into four lengths; each should measure 2m/6.5ft. Fold each length in half. Using a balanced pole, wall hook or nail as a support, drape the ropes together at the point of the fold so that all the rope ends hang down.

02

Make sure that the ropes are hanging at equal lengths. Gather the ropes together and tie one large knot, creating a large loop above the knot. This loop should be big enough to hang on the hook you choose to display the final planter.

03

Divide the eight strands of rope hanging below the knot into four pairs – separate them as they naturally fall so that each pair sits comfortably with its partnered rope.

04

Decide where you would like your first row of knots to sit – this should be roughly one quarter of the way below your top knot. These knots will sit above your plant. Tie a knot in each pair of ropes. They should be evenly placed so they line up when the ropes hang down; if they are uneven, simply loosen and adjust their position. To accommodate a larger plant pot, you may find it useful to keep this first row of knots high up the hanger.

05

Separate the ropes out below this row of knots, but this time use the left strand of rope from one pair and patch it to the right strand from the pair next to it. Once the ropes are in their new pairs, tie another row of knots slightly lower down. In this way, you will begin to create a mesh pattern, which will hold your plant pot securely.

06

Gather all of the ropes together, making sure they are not twisted and that there is no slack. Holding them with one hand, tie one final large knot, creating a secure base for your plant pot to rest on. Check that your plant pot sits comfortably inside the hanger and adjust the base knot if necessary. Finally, trim the ends of the rope to your desired length. Then add your plant.

AFTER WATERING, THE WEIGHT OF THE PLANT POT WILL INCREASE, SO MAKE SURE YOU HANG IT SOMEWHERE STABLE ENOUGH TO SUPPORT IT

VACANT CORNERS

{ depth, decor, diversity }

Where living space is limited, arranging a collection of potted plants in the corner of a room is a way of bringing the entire space to life. Since they are so diverse in leaf shape and height, and require less natural light than succulents, tropical plants are the perfect choice. By grouping them together, you can increase humidity and reduce their watering needs.

They grow quite quickly, so it is easy to encourage them to develop in a way that frames the space, whether trailing, climbing or standing in a selection of unique and various-sized pots. Use plant stands of varying heights to give a collection of plants some depth and interest and help to create an intense pocket of exotic greenery.

Just make a note of two simple things: after a time, you might need to gently bind longer stems to a supportive stick or pole to help them fill the space without collapsing. And you may also find it necessary to rotate plants in the corner of rooms so that one side is not always starved of light and the plant's leaves receive light evenly.

BELMORE SENTRY PALM

Kentian palm | Curly palm
Botanical Name *Howea belmoreana*
Family Arecaceae
Native To Lord Howe Island, Australia
Suggested Alternatives Parlour palm / Fishtail palm / Areca palm

Palms are fantastic houseplants, removing toxins from the air and giving generous amounts of fresh oxygen in return. With its elegant, arching leaves and slender stems, the Belmore sentry palm brings an instant hit of tropical paradise to any living room. Eventually growing up to 2½m/8ft tall, it is a long-term companion – but there is no need to be daunted as it grows very slowly and is very hardy if provided with its basic living needs.

LIGHT	This plant will tolerate shady conditions, but it prefers to be in bright, indirect light
TEMPERATURE	In the range of 15–24°C / 60–75°F and no cooler than 13°C / 55°F
WATERING	Keep the compost moist during spring and summer, allowing it to dry out between each watering during winter months. Mist the foliage regularly to ensure high humidity
FEEDING	Nourish with a liquid fertiliser every couple of weeks during spring and summer months
REPOTTING	Repot in mid-to-late spring every two or three years. Once it reaches the largest practical pot size, you can topdress its compost rather than repot it entirely
PROPAGATION	The sentry palm can only be grown from seed with the help of a heated propagator

---

CARE TIP | *If they become dull or dusty, you can clean this plant's leaves by standing it outside and giving it a shower with rainwater or a hose – but only do this on a warm day in spring or summer. Always remove dead leaves or stems with sharp scissors rather than by pulling to prevent stem damage.*

RUBBER PLANT

Indian rubber tree | Rubber fig
Botanical Name *Ficus elastica*
Family Moraceae
Native To India, China and Malaysia
Suggested Alternatives Fiddle-leaf fig / Dragon tree / Bengal fig

Few indoor plants are as easy to grow as the reliable rubber plant, which will eventually reach as tall as 3m/10ft. It is fantastically adaptable to different light and temperature conditions and happy in most rooms of the home. Its broad, intensely green and glossy leaves are just as beautiful on their underside, with a bright orange vein running from stem to tip. (Do note that this plant is toxic to dogs and cats if ingested.)

LIGHT	Place in indirect light, though a little direct light in the morning or afternoon is fine
TEMPERATURE	Ficus will gradually adapt to a range of indoor temperatures, but no cooler than 13°C / 55°F in winter
WATERING	Water moderately in spring and summer. Water enough to thoroughly wet its compost and then allow only the top 3cm/1½in to dry out in between each watering. An occasional misting is also a way of mimicking this plant's native tropical habitat. Reduce watering in the winter and keep an eye out for dropping leaves, which are an indication of overzealous watering
FEEDING	Feed with a liquid fertiliser every 3–4 weeks during spring and summer
REPOTTING	When necessary, repot in the spring into a pot only slightly larger than the original (about 5-10cm/2-4in larger), as it likes its roots to be fairly compact. Once it has grown into its largest practical pot size, you can top-dress its compost rather than repot it entirely
PROPAGATION	This species requires a high level of skill to propagate using the 'air layering' method – not recommended for the beginner gardener

---

HANDLING | *Be careful when handling or cleaning young leaves of this plant, since they are quite easily damaged and will remain so for the plant's entire life.*

OXALIS

Purple shamrock | Love plant
Botanical Name *Oxalis triangularis*
Family Oxalidaceae
Native To Tropical Brazil
Suggested Alternatives Lucky clover / Zebra plant / Friendship plant

Introduced to us by a friend, the oxalis has become one of our most treasured plants. Each of its delicate stems supports three butterfly shaped leaves, which beat in slow motion as they respond to the light: opening in the day and closing at night. Native to tropical Brazil, Mexico and South Africa (where it is considered by some to be a weed!), oxalis species have bulbous root systems that make them resilient to less-than careful owners. This dainty plant is commonly found in shades of deep purple or green, and blooms in clusters of little pink flowers in spring and summer.

LIGHT	Place in a location with lots of bright, indirect light. A little direct sunshine in the morning or afternoon is fine. Protect its leaves from strong midday sun in warmer months
TEMPERATURE	Oxalis will settle in warm or cool indoor conditions. Between 15–25°C / 59–77°F. Any higher will force it to keep itself alive by entering a dormant rest period
WATERING	Keep an eye on temperature conditions as these will affect how frequently you need to water. When watering, wet the compost of the oxalis thoroughly. Let the top 3cm/1½in dry out completely before watering again. Good drainage is key
FEEDING	The oxalis doesn't require much in the way of feeding, but you can add a little liquid fertiliser once every couple of months during spring and summer for an especially blooming plant
REPOTTING	Happy in a relatively small pot, but can be repotted in the spring once its roots become overcrowded. This will encourage it to spread outwards
PROPAGATION	Once it grows to a fairly large size, propagate by division (p111)

SOS WATERING | *The oxalis is miraculously adaptive: if neglected it will enter a state of forced rest. If you have left it unattended and find it dry and dead-looking, a good watering should revive its bulbs and new shoots should appear fairly quickly.*

Vacant Corners

MONSTERA

Swiss cheese plant / Ceriman / Fruit salad plant
Botanical Name *Monstera deliciosa*
Family Araceae
Native To Southern Mexico
Suggested Alternatives Calathea / Split leaf philodendron / Spider plant

The monstera is one of our absolute favourite plants to fill a corner, since it rewards you with an instant hit of luscious green with its heart-shaped, sprawling foliage and requires very little attention in return. Native to tropical rainforests, its naturally ribboned leaves are the plant's way of protecting itself from heavy rainfall. Although it is full of character and extremely resilient, note that the monstera is a fairly fast-growing species and will demand space as it matures.

LIGHT	Place in a position with bright, indirect light. Too much direct light can cause leaves to yellow, while too little light will prevent the leaves' signature cut-out holes from developing
TEMPERATURE	Between 18–24°C / 65–75°F during spring and summer, although it will tolerate slightly cooler or warmer conditions
WATERING	Water thoroughly only when the top 3cm/1½in of compost are dry. A regular misting will also keep the monstera happy if it is in a dry room
FEEDING	Feed with a liquid fertiliser once a month in spring and summer to encourage new and vibrant growth
REPOTTING	When its roots become crowded, repot in the spring. Use potting compost number 01 (p91)
PROPAGATION	Propagate in spring with stem cuttings (p106)

DISPLAYING | *You may need to use a moss pole for support as your monstera matures, gently tying the inner stems to the pole with twine or string. Alternatively, use string to bind the inner stems together and hold them upright.*

THE
BRIGHT SPOT

{ gather, bask, bloom }

With the sheer variety of desert cacti and succulents to fall in love with, it is lucky they are suited to being displayed together as a collective, all delighted to share a space in the brightest position in your home. Desert cacti and other succulents require similar lighting conditions, so you can confidently add to your collection of sun-loving species as you discover new favourites. We like to group very unusual-looking plants together for maximum interest and you can have fun finding different shaped pots and trays to match each one's personality.

In apartment living, where natural light is often limited, brightly lit windowsills and floors are often the most suitable choice. Just make a note that during their active growth period, you need to rotate each plant occasionally to ensure they get an even amount of the light that is coming from the window. And move them away from draughty windows in colder seasons to protect them from condensation and chilly temperatures.

JADE PLANT

Money tree | Lucky plant | Friendship tree
Botanical Name *Crassula ovata*
Family Crassulaceae
Native To South Africa
Suggested Alternatives Paddle plant / Red pagoda / Ripple jade

Considered a symbol of good luck, the hardy jade plant requires very little attention, is easy to propagate and eventually grows up to 1m/3ft tall if left untamed. The edges of its rubbery, oval leaves can turn red if placed in a spot where it can bathe in rays of direct sunlight and, given the right conditions, the plant may produce small, star-shaped flowers in early spring.

LIGHT
The plant will become misshapen in low lighting conditions and demands direct light in order to stand tall and proud. Make sure to rotate your plant every couple of weeks to encourage even growth

TEMPERATURE
Warm, dry conditions in the range of 18–24°C / 65–75°F during the day and cooler at night is fine

WATERING
Its compost should be allowed to dry out between each watering: once the top 3cm/1½in of its compost feels dry, water the plant quite generously, but never let its roots sit in water. Like other succulents, the jade plant requires very good drainage. Reduce watering in the winter, only doing so once its compost dries out completely

FEEDING
Nourish with a liquid fertiliser every three or four months during spring and summer

REPOTTING
Repot in spring only when its roots become crowded. Use potting compost 02 (p91). Go for a relatively shallow pot

PROPAGATION
Propagate with leaf cuttings (p102)

PRUNING | *If your jade plant begins to grow too tall, pinch or trim overgrown stems. This will control its size and encourage fullness lower down the plant.*

MEXICAN FIRECRACKER

Botanical Name *Echeveria setosa*
Family Crassulaceae
Native To Mexico
Suggested Alternatives *Echeveria elegans / Aeonium arboreum / Haworthia fasciata*

The Mexican firecracker is a sun-loving, star-shaped succulent which grows like other echeverias in a geometric rosette. Each juicy leaf is covered in soft, white hairs, which give the plant a shimmering appearance. Commonly found in hues of chalky green, blue and lilac, there are over a hundred species of echeveria, and they produce their colourful flowers on long stalks which shoot from the centre of their rosette of leaves, generally from late spring.

LIGHT	Find the sunniest place in your home for this firecracker and make sure it gets plenty of direct light
TEMPERATURE	Warm, dry conditions of around 18–24°C / 65–75°F during spring and summer and no cooler than 13°C / 55°F in winter
WATERING	Since they are native to dry, desert regions, these succulents like to be watered generously, but only once their soil is completely dry. Drainage is key, so use a watering tray and empty it a couple of hours after each watering
FEEDING	Feed with a liquid fertiliser every 3-4 weeks in spring and summer
REPOTTING	Repot in the spring when its roots become crowded. Add a layer of gravel at the base of its pot for drainage. Use potting compost 02 (p91)
PROPAGATION	Propagate with leaf cuttings in the spring and early summer (p102)

HANDLING | *Certain species of echeveria have a waxy coating on their leaves, which protects them from the harsh sunlight in the wild. Try not to touch leaves of these species when repotting, since they can easily be scratched and bruised.*

THE DESERT LANDSCAPE

Open container gardens are a great way to create a miniature desert scene, especially if you only have one really bright surface to display your favourite succulents. More elaborate than grouping potted plants, a container garden allows you to play with adding textured elements such as dried lichen, pieces of preserved wood and precious crystals and rocks, which add a magical dimension to the scene while breaking up the complex geometric forms of different desert-dwelling species of succulents.

Since desert cacti and succulents as a whole are slow-growing and require similar care, they work very well arranged together in one container. We try to include plants of different shapes, colours and textures to give each one its own focal point. For example, try contrasting juicy aloes with spiky cacti, colourful echeverias with hairy haworthias or low-lying lithops with sculptural euphorbias. Most importantly, pick plants that have similar needs for light, water and humidity so that the container is easy to care for as a whole.

When it comes to choosing a container, there are a few factors to keep in mind. These plants do not like to be enclosed and prefer to feel free surrounded by warm, dry air, so pick something relatively open. Try to select a watertight container (if you are using one made of wood, either apply a thin layer of polyurethane varnish or line the base with a sheet of plastic). Alternatively, a simple metal or plastic tray, dish or bowl will work too: young cacti and succulents have very shallow root systems, so the container doesn't have to be deep, around 10cm/4in. Our favourite places to find interesting containers are secondhand shops and flea markets, where we often uncover objects with a charming back story.

TOOLS AND MATERIALS

CONTAINER
FINE DRAINAGE STONES
ACTIVATED CHARCOAL
WOODEN SPOON
CACTI AND SUCCULENT COMPOST (P91)
SELECTION OF CACTI AND SUCCULENT PLANTS
DECORATIVE STONES AND ACCESSORIES
GARDENING GLOVES

01
Put on gardening gloves, if you like. Fill your container with stones to a depth of around 5cm/2in. Add a generous scattering of activated charcoal and mix it into the stones so that it is evenly distributed. This base will allow drainage for your plants, filtering any stagnant water and protecting their roots from sitting in water and developing rot.

02
For the next layer, add 5cm/2in of cacti and succulent compost. At this point it is a good idea to consider the final position of the container: you may want to rotate it as you begin planting to make sure the plants will be visible from the angle you are displaying the container. You can add different depths of compost in different sections of the container to create a more contoured scene.

03
Use your fingers, spoon or a small trowel to make a hole in the compost for your first plant to sit in. You can play around with positioning if the plant does not look right immediately. Secure compost around the plant's roots once you are happy with how it looks. Repeat with your next plant. Make sure to leave enough space between each plant to allow for some root growth and a good circulation of air. Gently press down the compost around each plant, removing any large air pockets, and secure them in their final positions.

04
Fill in any holes with extra compost. Add a final layer of drainage stones or other decorative elements to complete the scene. Once you have added all of your plants and decoration use a soft paintbrush to clean off any soil that may have collected on the plants.

05
Carefully water the entire surface with a spouted watering can or pipette. Make sure not to splash any leaves or stems. To determine when it is time to next water the container, check the moisture level of the soil with your finger and only water once it feels completely dry. Remember, desert cacti and other succulents are at their happiest in direct light, so choose the brightest spot in your home for your desert landscape, perhaps next to a window or under a skylight.

AFTER A FEW MONTHS, YOU MAY FIND THAT SOME PLANTS ARE GROWING WHILE OTHERS STAY SEEMINGLY UNCHANGED. YOU CAN PRUNE ANY OVERGROWN AREAS WITH SOME CLEAN, SHARP SCISSORS, EVENTUALLY REPLACING THOSE THAT OUTGROW THE CONTAINER. IF ANY PLANTS START TO SUFFER, SIMPLY REMOVE THEM AND REPLACE.

THE
WORK DESK

{ companions, calmers, distractors }

Whether your desk is a carefully arranged lesson in efficiency, or a charming clutter of accumulated objects and not-quite-completed projects, plants can be a wonderful companion to productivity. They offer a gentle reminder of the world outside, inspire moments of contemplation and provide a refreshing contrast to the technology that often surrounds us in our working environments.

If you work in a space where natural light is limited, larger tropical foliage plants such as ficus, palms and monstera can do very well in a position with indirect light. You can sit them on the floor or use a plant stand – it's a great way to add green to your working space without taking up a valuable corner on your desk. If you are fortunate enough to have good natural light, a couple of smaller potted succulents on your desk or lining your windowsills or shelves will shake things up. Wherever they go, they won't mind missing the occasional watering when you go on holiday and require very little maintenance.

FIDDLE-LEAF FIG

Botanical Name *Ficus lyrata*
Family Moraceae
Native To Western Africa
Suggested Alternatives Rubber plant / Monstera / Areca palm

With its elegant, viola-shaped leaves and sculptural silhouette, the fiddle-leaf is a gentle giant that will attract immediate attention wherever you place it. Crumpled and glossy, its densely packed leaves add the feeling of tropical paradise to any room blessed with bright natural light. More of a tree than a plant, the statuesque fiddle-leaf can grow up to 3m/10ft tall if regularly repotted, but the top branches can be lopped as desired once it reaches ceiling height.

LIGHT	In general, moderate to bright indirect light is best, but it will manage a little direct light in the morning or afternoon
TEMPERATURE	Between 18–24°C / 65–75°F in spring and summer. It will happily tolerate cooler conditions in the winter, but no lower than 13°C / 55°F
WATERING	Overwatering can cause serious damage, so make sure the top 3cm/1½in of the plant's compost is allowed to dry out between each watering. You should always try to use room temperature rainwater or filtered water to hydrate your plants, but that is especially the case with the sensitive ficus
FEEDING	Feed with a diluted liquid fertiliser once a month during spring and summer
REPOTTING	When its roots become crowded, repot in the spring into a pot not much bigger than the original (about 5cm/2in larger). Use potting compost 01 (p91)
PROPAGATION	This type of ficus is notoriously difficult to propagate so simply love the one you have

---

LEAF LOSS | *If you notice dropping leaves, this is most likely due to overwatering or too much dry air. Make sure the plant's soil is allowed to dry out in between watering and mist its leaves regularly in warmer months.*

STRING OF BEADS

Botanical Name *Senecio rowleyanus*
Family Asteraceae
Native To Namibia
Suggested Alternatives Wax vine / Stonecrop / Mistletoe cactus

This ornamental succulent looks very delicate but is in fact extremely hardy, requiring infrequent watering. It grows gradually, expanding its shower of bead-shaped leaves with little attention. Since it thrives in bright light, this low-maintenance species is suited to a sunny work desk, windowsill or hanging planter. You can let its stems grow and trail as long as 90cm/35in, or keep the plant compact by trimming them off and treating them as stem cuttings to propagate a brand new plant.

LIGHT	Place in a position with bright diffused or direct light
TEMPERATURE	Warm indoor conditions of around 18–24°C / 65–75°F are best during the active growth period in spring and summer. Aim for cooler winter conditions during its rest period (no lower than 10°C / 50°F), which will encourage it to flower in the spring
WATERING	Water it roughly once a month, or when the top 3cm/1½in of soil feels dry, making sure its roots never sit in water. Drainage is key for this plant's health
FEEDING	Nourish with a liquid fertiliser every two weeks in spring and summer
REPOTTING	When necessary, repot in the spring taking care not to knock its delicate stems. Use potting compost 02 (p91)
PROPAGATION	Propagate with stem cuttings in the spring and summer (p106)

REPOTTING | *This succulent is tricky to handle when repotting. Gently curl its stems around and upwards so that they are sitting on top of the compost and use the palm of one hand to hold them in place. You can then turn the plant upside down to release it from its pot and check if its roots are overcrowded.*

THE
BLANK CANVAS

{ adorn, embellish, transform }

Walls are often overlooked as good potential spaces to display plants. But more and more we see our friends invent clever ways of using walls to add new dimensions of green to their homes, whether that is by hanging dried wild-flower wreaths on hooks, or suspending air plants from pieces of delicate thread. In this way, even the smallest of living spaces can be brought to life with exotic forms.

If you are able to put up a couple of nails or ceiling hooks (without a landlord frowning disapprovingly), a wall hanging (p175), hanging planter (p135) or small shelf that is large enough for a couple of air plants are the simplest ways of adding a little pocket of wilderness to a room. Taking up very little space, these simple touches add a magical element of depth to an otherwise empty wall. Standing a plant in front of a mirror is another option, especially if you choose one as intricate and leafy as possible to create the illusion of twice as much tropical greenery.

CAPUT-MEDUSAE

Botanical Name *Tillandsia caput-medusae*
Family Bromeliaceae
Native To Forests of Mexico
Suggested Alternatives *Tillandsia capitata / Tillandsia circinata*

Meaning 'Head of Medusa', this plant looks a little like a Greek monster but is much more friendly in real life, with soft fuzzy leaves and long, pink and purple flowers while in bloom. It is found growing on trees in the forests of Mexico and South America, and its spiralling leaves can grow up to 40cm/16in high at full maturity. If you don't have a good space to hang your air plants, try placing them upright in a small pot, where their unusual appearance will instantly demand a closer look.

LIGHT	Lots of bright, filtered light mixed with a little direct light in the morning and afternoon. It will also survive fairly well in indirect light
TEMPERATURE	Between 18–30°C / 65–85°F will encourage the plant to flower. Avoid temperatures cooler than 12°C / 55°F
WATERING	Since it is native to humid forests, this species loves to be regularly and generously misted. Soak it once a week
FEEDING	Supplement the air plant's water with a weak dose of orchid fertiliser every couple of weeks during spring and summer
PROPAGATION	Like most air plants, the caput-medusae will produce new offsets, or 'pups', between the base of its leaves after it blooms. See p114 for more on propagation

POST-WATERING | *Since its base is so bulbous, the caput-medusae is prone to rot caused by a build-up of excess moisture. Make sure you let it dry fully after soaking (ideally upside down on a surface), before returning it to its display position.*

BULBOSA

Botanical name *Tillandsia bulbosa*
Family Bromeliaceae
Native To Southern Mexico, West Indies and Brazil
Suggested Alternatives *Tillandsia butzii* / *Tillandsia pseudobaileyi*

Brightly coloured and bulbous, the alien-looking bulbosa grows in a spiral of contorted leaves, and is easily propped up against a wall since its leaves are so long and sculptural. Its succulent-looking leaves store water, so it is a particularly good choice for children, or owners who might miss the occasional watering. This air plant has a particularly vibrant flowering cycle, blooming from its central scarlet rosette, and continuing to flower in violet for a few months before the flower eventually dries out.

LIGHT
This species of air plant responds to modest levels of natural light, so any shady to moderately bright, diffused light conditions are good

TEMPERATURE
Around 10–30°C / 50–85°F during the day and a cooler temperature at night is fine

WATERING
Native to damp forests and the shores of rivers, this species thrives in high humidity and therefore likes to be misted regularly. In warmer months, this can be as much as three times a week. If soaking, make sure that excess water is gently shaken off afterwards to prevent rot forming

FEEDING
You can feed the bulbosa every couple of weeks during its active growth period with a diluted orchid fertiliser by adding a few drops to its water

PROPAGATION
After flowering, the bulbosa begins to produce new plants at its base. These can be left attached to form an unusual-looking cluster of plants, or can be removed once they reach maturity to live independently as new plants. See p114 for more on propagating

---

DISPLAYING | *If you position your bulbosa air plant upright on a shelf or wall hanging, make sure to let it dry on its side or upside down after watering to prevent excess moisture sitting between its leaves and causing rot.*

THE FORAGED WALL HANGING

Many of the materials we use in our planter and hanger designs were inspired by our travels, from the intricately patterned balls of Moroccan marble we began using as terrarium bottle stoppers, to crystallised minerals and silky driftwood from the coasts of England. Like weathered souvenirs of each landscape, they seem to bring a bit of tactile life to our indoor displays and evoke memories of faraway adventures.

For this design you will only need three base materials: a nail, some rope and a piece of wood. If you have a drill, you can make a couple of holes in the wood to attach your rope, but otherwise you can simply tie the rope instead.

This project is all about simplicity, so do not worry if you find yourself improvising with other available materials. Thread, fabric or string can be used in the place of rope and, if you prefer, you can replace the driftwood with a piece of shop-bought wooden dowel or a length of hollow copper metal pipe.

Air plants are the ideal choice for decorating a wall hanging as they generally prefer indirect light and can easily be moved when it comes to watering. But think about adding a few ornamental elements to your wall hanging and make it personal to you.

TOOLS AND MATERIALS

DRIFTWOOD
ROPE, STRING OR THREAD
NAIL OR PICTURE HOOK
HAMMER
DRILL (OPTIONAL)
AIR PLANTS
FOUND OBJECTS

01

If you are going to use a drill to make holes for your rope, use a pencil to mark a place at either end of the piece of wood where you would like the rope to be positioned. Drilling holes is not essential for this design, so if you do not have access to a drill, or have never used one before, ignore this step and move straight to step 03. If the wood is warped or curved, hold it against the wall to decide which way you would like it to hang before drilling any holes.

02

Depending on the thickness of the rope or thread you are using, choose a suitably sized drill bit for wood. Find an outdoor surface you can rest the driftwood on. Position the end of wood you are drilling so it is sticking out over the edge of the surface, and hold the driftwood firmly with one hand, keeping hand and fingers well away from the area you are about to drill. Carefully drill the first hole all the way through the wood. Repeat on the other side. Once finished, thread each end of your rope through the holes and tie a knot, giving each one a tug to check it will hold.

03

If you are not making holes in the wood, simply tie your rope to either side of the wood, keeping in mind how low you would like it to hang below the nail. Have a play with different ways to tie the rope; you can make the knots as simple or detailed as you like. Give the knots a tug after you finish tying them to make sure they will hold.

04

When the rope is attached securely to both ends of the wood, your wall hanging can be suspended from a hook or nail. Once hung, you can begin to add the air plants and other objects of your choice, positioning them along the wood in your own unique design.

IF YOU ARE STRUGGLING TO BALANCE YOUR AIR PLANTS OR FORAGED OBJECTS, SIMPLY USE SOME CLEAR FISHING WIRE OR DELICATE THREAD TO GENTLY ATTACH EACH ONE TO THE HANGING. REMEMBER, YOU CAN MIST YOUR AIR PLANTS WEEKLY TO KEEP THEM HEALTHY, BUT THEY WILL BENEFIT FROM AN OCCASIONAL SOAKING, SO TRY NOT TO TIE THEM ON TOO TIGHTLY.

THE IMMORTAL COMPANION

{ spirited, resilient, faithful }

Unfortunately, all indoor plants will die if you ignore their needs for long enough, but there are some that will keep bouncing back no matter what life (or their owner) throws at them. On the following pages we have chosen three plants that will tolerate periods of neglect, draught and darkness. Recommended for the frequent traveller, the forgetful plant-lover and the clumsy indoor gardener, these reliable plants are likely to survive against the odds.

We have chosen the plants for different reasons, so it is still important to check why each one is so low-maintenance. For example, the snake plant (p183) and fern leaf cactus, which are each particularly resilient to a missed watering or two, may die if overwatered in winter months.

Once you have identified which kind of plants might survive your lifestyle and living conditions, you can begin to bring them into your home with the confidence that they won't fill you with guilt by looking upset or needy if you fail to show them how much you love them.

ZZ PLANT

Zanzibar gem | Eternity palm
Botanical name *Zamioculcas zamiifolia*
Family Araceae
Native To Southern and Eastern Africa
Suggested Alternatives Sago palm / Rubber plant / Clusia

Absent-minded indoor garden enthusiasts: this is the plant for you. The ZZ needs very little light, survives long periods of neglect and is immune to many pests which can affect other house plants. Its naturally vigorous and polished-looking leaves can flower in bronze during summer and autumn – its 'stems' are actually leaves growing directly from the ground and from these grow emerald green, glossy leaflets in pairs. Indoors, the plant can grow up to 60cm/24in tall, eventually looking more like a miniature tropical tree.

LIGHT	It prefers lots of bright, indirect light, but it will also survive in much lower lighting conditions if it can get a little light in the morning or afternoon. Keep it protected from harsh midday sun if you live in a warmer climate
TEMPERATURE	Around 18-26°C / 65-79°F will encourage leaf growth and keep this plant at its optimum health. It will also tolerate cooler conditions, but no lower than 15°C / 59°F
WATERING	Overwatering is this plant's biggest killer as its bulbous tubers are vulnerable to rot caused by a build-up of excess moisture. Water only when the top 3cm/1½in of its compost are completely dry, and ensure good drainage
FEEDING	Feed with a 1 part liquid fertiliser to 4 parts water once a month in spring and summer
REPOTTING	When necessary, repot in the spring. Use potting compost 01 (p91)
PROPAGATION	Propagate with stem cuttings (p106) in spring and summer, but they may take as much as a year to show new growth

---

LITTLE ONES & CURIOUS PAWS | *This plant is not recommended for people with inquisitive pets or very young children, since it can cause stomach upsets if eaten.*

SNAKE PLANT

Mother-in-law's tongue | Good luck plant | Devil's tongue
Botanical Name *Sansevieria trifasciata*
Family Asparagaceae
Native To Southern and Western Africa
Suggested Alternatives Spider plant / Peace lily / Cast iron plant

This forgiving plant will withstand even the most irresponsible of botanical enthusiasts, is tolerant of missed watering, will survive in almost any lighting conditions and rarely needs repotting. Growing slowly during its active growth period, the snake plant's vertical leaves are distinctly patterned in marbled shades of green, sometimes with golden edges, and they require no pruning.

LIGHT	Although it prefers bright light, the snake plant is very amenable to both light or shade
TEMPERATURE	Native to the tropics of Nigeria and the Congo, the snake plant revels in the warmth, around 18–26°C / 65–79°F, with a minimum winter temperature of 13°C / 55°F
WATERING	In spring and summer, water moderately, thoroughly wetting the potting soil and allowing the top 3cm/1½in to dry out in between each watering. Overwatering, particularly in the winter, can be lethal
FEEDING	Feed with a diluted liquid fertiliser once a month during spring and summer
REPOTTING	This plant's roots are healthiest when left crowded and it only needs to be repotted every few years in early spring. In between pottings, topdress by replacing the top layer of the plant's soil with fresh compost
PROPAGATION	Propagate in spring by division (p111)

TOXIN TAKER | *Not only is the snake plant as resilient as houseplants come, it also efficiently cleanses the air from harmful toxins found indoors.*

FISHBONE CACTUS

Ric rac cactus | Zigzag cactus
Botanical Name *Epiphyllum anguliger*
Family Cactaceae
Native To Mexico
Suggested Alternatives Fern leaf cactus / orchid cactus / Easter cactus

With a silhouette like no other, the wonderfully wiggly fishbone cactus instantly transforms an empty space and in return asks for very little. Since its succulent, toothy-looking leaves are so widespread, it works well when placed in a central spot of a living room, or suspended in a hanging planter. Found growing in groups in the tropical rainforests of Mexico, this epiphyte species blooms its fragrant white and pale pink flowers at night-time during spring and summer.

LIGHT	Since it is used to dappled sunshine in its native environment, this plant prefers bright, indirect light, and a little direct light in the morning and afternoon if possible.
TEMPERATURE	Indoor temperatures around 12-20°C / 55-70°F. Keep this plant in cooler indoor conditions during winter months, which will encourage a period of rest and lead to healthy growth in spring and summer
WATERING	In spring and summer months, when the top 3cm/1½in of its soil is completely dry, give it a generous amount of water, pouring away any excess from its drainage tray after a few hours. Reduce in the winter, only watering when all the plant's soil is thoroughly dried out
FEEDING	Feed with liquid fertiliser once a month in spring and summer, as this will encourage it to flower
PROPAGATION	Propagate in the spring with leaf cuttings (p102)

HANDLING | *Although they are very fine, the spines of many forest cacti can easily penetrate the skin and can be quite irritating. Wear gloves when handling them, especially if transferring them into a hanging planter.*

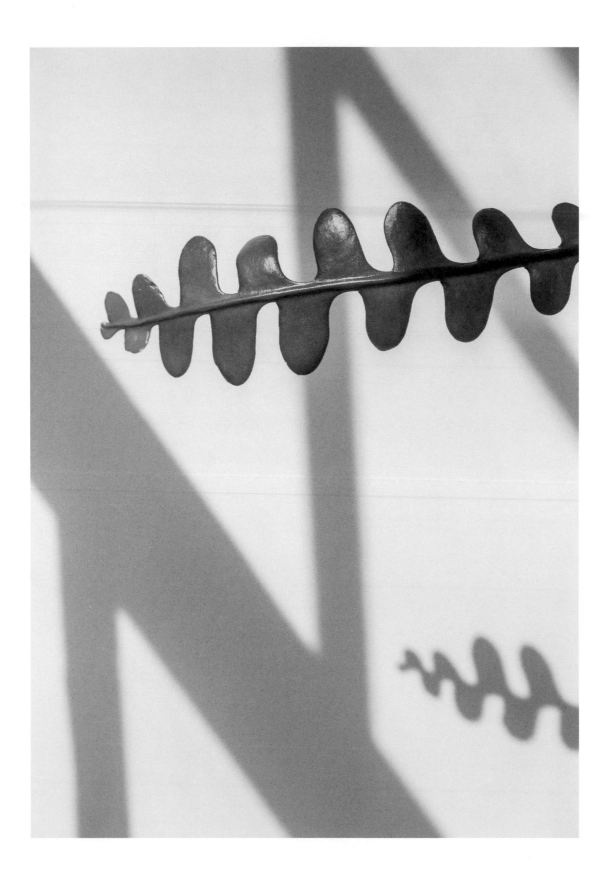

STRANGE
SURFACES

{ mischievous, unique, unusual }

We believe that even the smallest of rooms can accommodate an unexpected hit of tropical enchantment. With no tables, shelves or windowsills free to use, an unusual plant arranged on a corner chair, bedside stool or stack of books can add an exotic focal point while making the most of limited surface space.

A strange surface calls for a strange plant and we have featured two of our all-time favourite oddballs; both will instantly draw the attention of anyone in a room. In a bright home, trailing cacti such as the monkey's tail or species of rhipsalis are a winning choice and will bloom in pink and red flowers in the spring. For spaces with less natural sunlight, flowering species from the weird and wonderful family of bromeliads will happily sit on a surface dappled with indirect light.

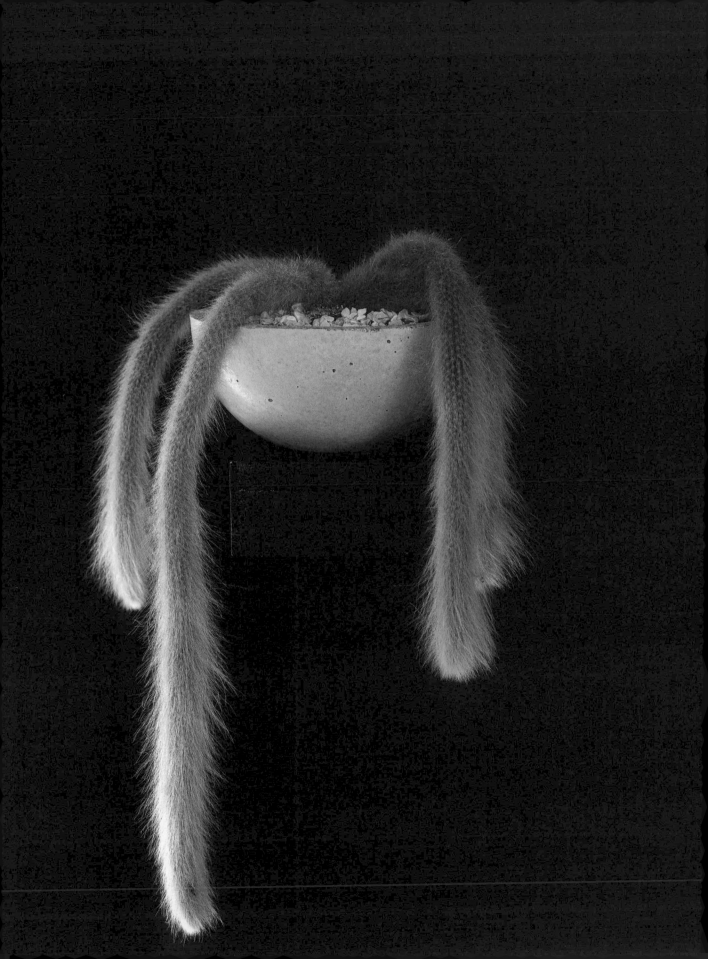

MONKEY'S TAIL CACTUS

Botanical Name *Hildewintera colademononis / Cleistocactus colademononis*
Family Cataceae
Native To Bolivia
Suggested Alternatives Chain cactus / Mistletoe cactus

This fluffy cactus is found growing from branches and steep cliffs in mountainous areas of Santa Cruz in Bolivia, where its trailing stems can grow up to 2½m/8ft long and are covered in a thick layer of hairy spines that protect the plant from the harshest summer sunshine. It is best placed where it will receive a good amount of fresh air. In the spring, your photogenic companion should shock you with a surreal flush of orange, pink and red flowers that bloom in patterns along the length of its stems.

LIGHT	This species requires bright, direct light, where it will glow in a haze of fuzzy fur
TEMPERATURE	In warmer months, any normal room temperature is suitable. In winter, around 10–12°C/50 54°F to encourage a period of rest
WATERING	Water generously in spring and summer only when the top 3cm/1½in of the plant's soil is completely dry, but ensure good drainage. Reduce watering in autumn and winter, only doing so when its soil is dry throughout
FEEDING	You can feed the monkey's tail cactus every two weeks during the active growth period to encourage flowering
REPOTTING	When necessary, repot after flowering into a pot only slightly larger than the original. Use potting compost 02 (p91)
PROPAGATION	Propagate with 15cm tip cuttings in late spring or early summer and treat as offsets (p114–116)

HANDLING | *Contrary to its gentle appearance, the fine spines of this cactus are quick to shed when handled and can cause irritation to the skin. Wear a thick pair of gloves when touching it and position it so it won't be brushed against.*

URN PLANT

Silver vase | Scarlet star
Botanical Name *Aechmea fasciata*
Family Bromeliaceae
Native To Brazil
Suggested Alternatives Pineapple plant / Guzmania / Flaming sword

This show-stopping bromeliad is found growing on the floor of Brazilian rainforests, where moisture collects within its tough, silvery-green mottled leaves in a watertight inner 'vase'. After around five years, it produces a single, central bract, which flowers in bright pink and violet for many months. Keep in mind that this plant dies after it flowers, so only buy a flowering specimen if you are happy to either propagate its offsets or replace it within six months.

LIGHT	Like many bromeliads, this plant prefers bright, indirect light, but little direct sunshine in the morning or afternoon should be fine
TEMPERATURE	Around 18–24°C / 65–75°F will keep this plant healthy and encourage flowering. Temperatures can be slightly cooler at night and in winter
WATERING	Water by filling and topping up the inner rosette, roughly once or twice a month. Rainwater is preferred, but not essential. Only ever water the compost when the top 3cm/1½in feels completely dry. An occasional misting is also welcomed
FEEDING	During spring and summer months, add a little diluted liquid fertiliser to the compost once a month
REPOTTING	If you buy a flowering plant, there is no need to move it from its pot. If it is not flowering, repot in spring when its roots become crowded. Use potting compost 01 (p91)
PROPAGATION	After flowering, this plant produces offsets, at which point the parent plant reaches the end of its growth cycle and begins to die, acting as a reserve of nutrients to the young plants. Offsets should only be removed in summer months once they grow to around 10cm/4in, and then be repotted into a moist compost. See p114 for more on propagation

LITTLE HANDS

{ playing, learning, nurturing }

The best thing about working on a market stall is the continuous flow of people you meet each day: happy, relaxed people of all ages enjoying time wandering and exploring. It is a wonderful atmosphere in which to have conversations with our customers, and one thing we learnt early on was: children are utterly enthralled by unusual plants.

There are many reasons why indoor plants are beneficial to children, from giving them a glimpse of the wonders of botany to teaching them the satisfaction of caring for another living thing, particularly when pets are not an option. It is amazing to see a child's innate desire to nurture, and often we see a little hand emerge from below eye-level towards a row of cacti before being gently batted away by an amused parent.

Some plants are less likely to survive at the hands of an enthusiastic child, but others make brilliant companions. Softer cacti are the practical choice, since they are such slow growers and resilient to a bit of manhandling. The donkey tail sedum is especially easy to propagate and can be used for experiments with growing new plants. Air plants are also an easy, mess-free option, but require a little more care.

DONKEY TAIL

Burro's tail | Lamb's tail | Horse's tail
Botanical Name *Sedum morganianum*
Family Crassulaceae
Native To Southern Mexico
Suggested Alternatives Golden sedum / Jade plant / Rosary vine

We first discovered this juicy sedum in the hidden oasis of the Barbican Conservatory in London, where it appeared as a waterfall of boat-shaped leaves, blooming in rusty pink, crown-shaped flowers. It looks best displayed in a hanging planter or over the edge of a bright bookshelf or windowsill. This plant's pendant stems are an explosion of colour, eventually growing up to 1m/3ft long in ombré shades of dusty green and blue. Since these leaves shed so easily, it is the perfect plant with which to practise propagating with children.

LIGHT	Sedums love direct light, which deepens the colouring of the plant's fleshy leaves and encourages flowering in the summer. Too little light can cause their stems to weaken
TEMPERATURE	Around 15–24°C / 60–75°F and no cooler than 13°C / 55°F at night or in winter
WATERING	Thoroughly wet the soil when watering, but allow the top 3cm/1½in to dry out before watering again. Overwatering will damage this plant quickly, especially during autumn and winter. During its rest period in winter, let the soil dry out completely in between each watering and make sure your pot has good drainage
FEEDING	Sedums do not require regular feeding to thrive
REPOTTING	Repot when necessary in the spring. Handle this plant with care, since its leaves are very delicate. Use potting compost 02 (p91)
PROPAGATION	Propagate in the spring or summer with leaf cuttings (p102)

OLD MAN CACTUS

Bunny cactus | White Persian cat cactus
Botanical Name *Cephalocereus senilis*
Family Cactaceae
Native To Mexico
Suggested Alternatives Silver torch cactus / Snowball cactus / Powder puff cactus

The old man cactus is a characterful chap, columnar in shape once mature and vertically ribbed underneath its striking coat of coarse hair that protects it from frost. Notably hardy, it is native to the arid regions of Mexico, where it can grow for hundreds of years and up to 15m/50ft tall. Perhaps reassuringly, it is unlikely to fully mature indoors, though it may produce its trumpet-shaped, magenta flowers once it has been with you for 10 to 20 years.

LIGHT
Since its hairs protect it from the harshest sunlight in the wild, this cactus adores being in constant light. Too little light may cause it to grow with thinning hair and an unnaturally elongated stem

TEMPERATURE
Between 10–30°C / 50–85°F in spring and summer, and slightly cooler during its rest period in autumn and winter

WATERING
Water whenever the top 3cm/1½in feels dry during spring and summer. In its rest period, water only once its soil is dry throughout. Like all cacti, too much water in the autumn and winter can lead to rotting, so never place it in a room with high humidity

FEEDING
Feed with a cactus fertiliser once a month, being careful not to splash and discolour its hairs

REPOTTING
Like most slow-growing succulents, this cactus will require repotting in the spring only once its roots are visible at the edge of its soil. Take care when handling, since its deceptively soft hair conceals sharp little spines

PROPAGATION
This species requires advanced techniques for propagation

CLEANING | *If your old man cactus picks up pieces of dust or soil, clean it with a soft, dry paintbrush.*

THE
GATHERING

arrange, share and celebrate
in a house of plants

Our journey with plants was inspired by the need to feel connected – not just to the natural world, but also to other places and people. By going out and collecting plants and objects that inspired us, and then bringing them together to share with those we met and worked with, we found we could engage with the world around us, reach new people and find common ground with our existing friends. A sense of community evolved, encouraging us to explore, experiment and share even more.

We learned that plants create a sense of familiarity and welcoming in a home or public space – and they also encourage reflection. In moments of careful focus, particularly during the workshops we run, the plants seemed to highlight the value of working in a slow and considered way.

But they are also decorative, entertaining and even life-affirming – sitting with friends in the evening glow of candlelight, the shadows of a towering palm reaching out protectively over the half-empty plates, seems like the ultimate celebration of life. Whether for a birthday, wedding or a simple weekend dinner, elements of greenery are a wonderful way to create an imaginative space to get lost in for a few precious hours. By bringing hints of plant-life to the table, those moments can become even more special.

Perhaps that is the answer: green encourages us out into the world to explore, and then it brings us home to a place of sanctuary.

XEROGRAPHICA

Giant air plant | Silver queen
Botanical Name *Tillandsia xerographica*
Family Bromeliaceae
Native To Guatemala
Suggested Alternatives *Tillandsia caput-medusae | Tillandsia capitata* 'Peach'

Known to live for up to 25 years, the regal-looking xerographica is one of the only air plant species to thrive in direct light, and can be kept outside in warmer seasons. This sculptural, silvery-green plant produces a single, violet-coloured flower with each bloom cycle. An extremely slow-growing epiphyte, the xerographica is also incredibly hardy and can be displayed by suspending it from a fine rope, or placing it on a surface or bowl.

LIGHT	Direct light is preferred, but it will also survive fairly well with plenty of indirect light
TEMPERATURE	Between 10–30°C / 50–85°F throughout the year is fine
WATERING	Mist or soak once a week in room temperature water. Make sure to gently shake off any excess moisture after watering to prevent rot forming inside its leaves. Exaggerated curvature of its leaves will tell you when the plant is dehydrated and needs more frequent watering
FEEDING	Nourish the xerographica with an air plant fertiliser mixed with its water every few weeks in the spring and summer
PROPAGATION	Each plant will produce up to eight new plants in its life. These offsets are commonly called 'pups', and grow between the parent plant's leaves. Once they are about a quarter of the size of the parent plant, they can be gently removed after a generous soaking. See p114 for more on propagating

---

CARE TIP | *Make sure your xerographica receives fresh air to prevent moisture building up in its leaves and becoming stagnant.*

OAXACANA

Botanical Name *Tillandsia oaxacana*
Family Bromeliaceae
Native To Mexico
Suggested Alternatives *Tillandsia magnusiana / Tillandsia plagiotropica*

Discovered in the Mexican state of Oaxaca, the star-shaped oaxacana air plant has soft, chalky green leaves that fade from light to dark green as they develop and fan outwards. Each leaf is coated in silvery fuzz, which makes this plant particularly soft to the touch. One of the hardier species we have found, it grows up to 20cm/8in at full maturity and produces distinctive, violet and yellow flowers when it blooms.

LIGHT	Place in bright, indirect light. Too much direct sunlight can cause its leaves to curl and dry out, eventually killing it
TEMPERATURE	Between 10-30°C / 50-85°F and cooler during the night
WATERING	In warmer months, the oaxacana requires a generous misting or soaking at least once weekly with room temperature water. Like all air plants, make sure to gently shake off any excess water afterwards to prevent rot forming within its dense leaves. Look out for excessive curling of this plant's leaves, which indicates that it is dehydrated
FEEDING	Nourish this species with a diluted orchid fertiliser every few weeks by adding a few drops to its water during spring and summer
PROPAGATION	Air plants produce new plants in between the base of their leaves once they reach maturity. Once these offsets are around two thirds the size of the parent plant, they can be gently removed after softening with a generous soaking. See p114 for more on propagating

---

PRUNING | *Do not be alarmed if the outermost leaves become dry and loose. New leaves are produced from the plant's centre and older leaves can be pruned by gently tweaking them off.*

SPANISH MOSS

Old man's beard | Beard lichen
Botanical Name *Tillandsia usneoides*
Family Bromeliaceae
Native To Subtropical regions including Florida, South America and Chile

The most widely found air plant in the wild, Spanish moss is a true epiphyte and grows densely in treetops in delicate swathes up to a length of 6m/20ft. From mid-spring, it produces tiny, lime green, fragrant flowers. This simple and ethereal air plant looks striking styled in feathery bundles, and works well trailing from a hook, curtain pole or placed in a pot to hang over a windowsill or bookshelf. Since it is so soft and flexible, we often use it to decorate a dinner party table, but it prefers to grow hanging straight down.

LIGHT	Spanish moss grows well in bright or shady environments, but does not like direct sunlight
TEMPERATURE	This species will tolerate a range of temperatures, from very warm to cool indoor conditions. However, avoid moving it once acclimatised as it will not respond well to sudden changes in its living conditions
WATERING	Since its leaves are so thin, Spanish moss is prone to dehydration and prefers to be in a place with high humidity. To keep it healthy, mist it regularly, as much as once every day in the warmest months, and soak it once a week. Use rain or filtered water if possible
FEEDING	Feed with a little orchid fertiliser mixed in a misting bottle during spring and summer months to encourage flowering
PROPAGATION	This species will self-propagate and multiply quite quickly if given ideal living conditions, especially if divided into smaller bundles in summer months

SPOTTING DEHYDRATION | *If you are unsure how often to water your Spanish moss, check its colour. It is a light and silvery shade of green when dry, and will turn a darker shade of green when it is thoroughly hydrated.*

HIMMELI

From the Swedish word 'himmel' meaning 'heaven' or 'sky', himmelis were originally created in rural Nordic areas to celebrate the beginning of the Winter Solstice. Made from rye straw from the previous year's harvest, the completed mobiles were suspended inside the house as good luck charms for the future.

We first began designing the mobiles as a way to suspend our favourite air plants, finding the little geometric structures a striking way to make the most of limited surface space. By cutting different lengths of straw and threading them together with wire, we discovered an endless range of shapes to experiment with. This simple himmeli can be hung from a delicate ceiling hook or placed on a surface. Wire is the easiest way to thread the straws together as it is fairly rigid, but a needle and thread will do the job just as well.

Once you have tried making this simple diamond shape, you can start to design your own, more intricate mobiles. We suggest starting with a flat shape such as a square or hexagon, and then adding straws above and below, from joint to joint, to begin creating a unique, three-dimensional structure.

To water your air plant, remove it from the himmeli and either mist or soak it in room temperature water. After watering, gently shake off any excess water, allow it to dry and return it to the himmeli.

01

Measure out 1½m/5ft of wire and cut to length. You will need four straws that measure 7cm/2¾in, and eight straws that measure 10cm/4in. Little differences in length will not matter too much, but may cause the final shape to be slightly warped.

02

Thread the four 7cm/2¾in straws together to form a square, knotting to secure once you have threaded it through all four straws. You can lay the square on a flat surface for the next step.

03

Starting on one side of the square, thread two of the 10cm/4in straws on to the wire. Making sure there is no slack in the wire, knot the end of the second straw to the next corner of the square, forming a triangular wing. Thread the wire through to the other side of the square. Repeat this step on the opposite side of the square.

04

Bring the two triangular wings together so they meet, and secure the tips of the two triangles together by threading the wire up to the top of one, and looping it around the tip of the other.

05

Thread the wire back down to one corner of the square, and, using the final four 10cm/4in straws, repeat steps 3 and 4.

06

Using the remaining wire, you can now suspend your himmeli in your chosen spot. If using the mobile as a plant holder, remember that air plants thrive in bright, indirect light.

ONCE YOU HAVE PRACTISED, TRY USING OTHER MATERIALS SUCH AS
LENGTHS OF CUT COPPER, BRASS OR OTHER METAL TUBES. THE LIGHTER THE
MATERIAL YOU PICK, THE MORE INTRICATE YOU CAN MAKE EACH MOBILE.

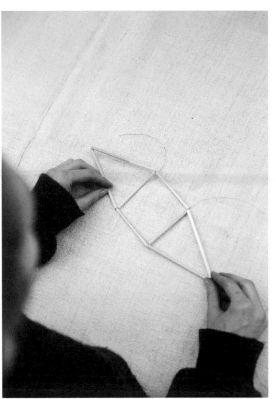

INDEX

Page numbers in **bold** indicate a main section.

THANK YOU

To our families and our parents – Jane & Keith Ray and Fiona & Richard Langton – for their generosity, patience and solid support. And to Grandma Ann, for her house of plants. This book is for you.

To our commissioning editor Zena Alkayat, who guided and encouraged us at every step.

To photographer Erika Raxworthy, talented capturer of overlooked details, who calmly added her magical touch and whose photography played a big part in the extra 32 pages we added to the book at the last minute.

To Alicia Galer for illustrating the house and plants with such colour and character, and to Luke Fenech for his help with art direction, for designing the pages and bringing them to life.

To all of our brilliant friends, many of whom contributed directly to this book. In particular to Caroline Wilkinson, Olivia Fox, Fiongal Greenlaw, Kezia Regan and Petor Georgallou.

To those who helped us with our research: Mark and Amanda Smith from Key Essentials for their valuable advice on air plant care, and Bryan and Linda Goodey from the incredible Cactus Land at Southfield Nurseries for a feline-supervised lesson in cacti botany we will never forget. A huge thank you to Gareth Hopcroft, protected horticulturalist and specialist in hydroponics, for his time and generosity and for letting us share his compost recipes. And further thanks to Laura Nicolson and Nancy Marten.

We were fortunate enough to collaborate with a group of talented designers in the making of this book, many who generously created bespoke items for us. Thank you to Alex Devol from Wooden & Woven, Luke Hope from Hope in the Woods and John Shorrock for the hand-carved homeware and terrarium tools. To William Edmonds and Charlotte McLeish for their ceramics, and Lora Avedian for her intricate paper plants.

To the people who donated their homes and work spaces: Eva Coppens at Forest London and Holly Wulff Petersen. Special thanks to Benedicte Sartorio who welcomed us into her home and inspired us with her eye for interior design, colour and detail.

For kindly lending us props to help with the styling: Jack and Maya from Rospo and M.i.h for their clothes, Bloomingville for their homeware and Grafa for their beautiful gardening tools. To Hazel Stark for letting us steal her avocado plant, which we have not yet returned...

House of Plants
Copyright © 2016 Quarto Publishing plc.
Text copyright © Caro Langton & Rose Ray
Photographs copyright © Erika Raxworthy
Illustrations copyright © Alicia Galer
Design: Luke Fenech
Commissioning editor: Zena Alkayat

First published in 2016 by Frances Lincoln,
an imprint of The Quarto Group
The Old Brewery, 6 Blundell Street
London N7 9BH, United Kingdom
www.QuartoKnows.com

All rights reserved.
No part of this publication may be reproduced,
stored in a retrieval system, or transmitted, in any
form, or by any means, electronic, mechanical,
photocopying, recording or otherwise without the
prior written permission of the publisher or a licence
permitting restricted copying. In the United Kingdom
such licences are issued by the Copyright Licensing
Agency, Barnards Inn, 86 Fetter Lane, London,
EC4A 1EN.

A catalogue record for this book is available
from the British Library.

ISBN 978-0-7112-3837-4

Printed and bound in China

4 5 6 7 8 9

FRANCES LINCOLN

Brimming with creative inspiration, how-to projects and useful
information to enrich your everyday life, Quarto Knows is a favourite
destination for those pursuing their interests and passions. Visit our
site and dig deeper with our books into your area of interest: Quarto
Creates, Quarto Cooks, Quarto Homes, Quarto Lives, Quarto Drives,
Quarto Explores, Quarto Gifts, or Quarto Kids.